FOCUS

THE ART OF CLEAR THINKING

In Memory of my Mother's Magic
One of Short Influence with Long Impact

FOCUS

THE ART OF CLEAR THINKING

VALERIE PIERCE

MERCIER PRESS
Irish Publisher – Irish Story

MERCIER PRESS

Cork

www.mercierpress.ie

ISBN: 978 1 78117 204 9

10 9 8 7 6 5 4 3 2 1

Printed and bound in the EU.

CONTENTS

Concentrate all your thoughts upon the work at hand.
The sun's rays do not burn until brought to a focus.

Alexander Graham Bell

Part 1

Focus: Why Bother?

1

BEGINNING AT THE SOURCE

I was four and a half years old when I learned to focus in the dark without being afraid.

Focus fights your Fears

I was six, almost seven years old, when I learned how exciting it felt to focus on challenging myself to succeed.

Focus is Fun

I was eight years old when my mother, who showed me these lessons, died … and it was at eight years of age that I realised, with the wonderful support of a strong and loving father, I could carry these lessons with me for the rest of my life.

Focus is Forever

Focus is natural: we are born with an instinct to focus on exactly what we want and a very strong pair of lungs to help us get it. Then, somewhere along the line, as we grow up and life gets complicated, many of us begin to lose that focus as we become overwhelmed by choice and information. We can lose that essential skill which we need to achieve what we want, when we want it.

The art of Clear Thinking is the skill to be able to see what you want and Focus is the ability to develop the strength of willpower, self-discipline and intellectual savvy to achieve it.

So how do we do this? Let me first tell you these stories from my early experiences by way of illustration, before we begin the task of learning what type of thinking techniques and skills you will use to achieve successful Focus.

Let's start with the first story.

FOCUS FIGHTS YOUR FEARS

I remember as a small child being terrified to walk across a very large landing in our house in the dark, something that was necessary for me to do to get from my bedroom to the bathroom. To help me to overcome my night-time fear, my mother very gently and deliberately made me focus on each piece of furniture on that landing in daylight. We touched each item and noticed where they were positioned – the telephone table, the chair, the chest of drawers, etc. We also focused on the railing of the stairway and the two steps I had to walk over to reach the bathroom. Then, at night-time, with the light off, we went through the same routine of touching the same furniture and noticing the placement of all the items I would meet on my way to the bathroom.

Then in the dark, my mother asked me to focus on the fact that everything we touched and felt was exactly the same as it was when I could see it in daylight. 'There, you see,' I remember her saying. 'Nothing has changed on this landing. Everything is the same, both in daylight and in the dark. If you are not afraid to walk through this landing in the daytime – and I know how much you love playing here with your friends – then there is no need to be afraid at night-time, because this space is exactly the same. The only thing that has changed here is you. It is your fears that are making you afraid, not the landing; there is nothing to be afraid of once you know your way. You know you can be safe.'

I remember those words always – *there is nothing to be afraid of once you know your way*, once you focus on your direction. Thinking clearly and with a solid focus on our goals helps us to achieve our desires.

Of course, as an adult, I realise I was no longer frightened in the dark because something *had* changed in that scenario – my *perception* of my situation. I now understand that in the daylight I felt in control as I could see where I was going; in the dark I lost that control because I could not. So Clear Focus and knowledge of where we are going helps control our emotions in a useful way – conversely, lack of focus and lack of direction can evoke destructive emotions, such as fear, that can hinder our way. The lesson is that there is no need to be frightened of your own perceptions. We can control our awareness, our beliefs and how we make sense of a situation, so that our thinking and feelings can work for us and not against us. The aim of this book is to show you how.

Focus is not always associated with hard work and tough feelings. It can also give us some of the greatest pleasures in our lives, and can be fun. By way of illustration let me tell you how I learned this at the tender age of almost seven years, with my second story of motherly wisdom.

FOCUS IS FUN

I call this 'The Story of the Stones'.

At the front of our house was a lovely gravelled garden. I remember as a child sitting on the window ledge enjoying the warmth of the sun while creating designs in the pebbles with my feet. It was one of my favourite places to sit and watch the world go by on our village square.

One day my mother began to play a little game with me: to see how long it took me to fill a small biscuit tin with pebbles. The idea was to put a stone into the box *only* whenever I overcame a particular challenge or 'an act of self-denial' as she called it. Looking back, this was an excellent way to teach a child 'delayed gratification', an essential requirement for success in adult life.

In fact you may well know the story of the 'marshmallow' experiment in the 1960s, in which scientists at Stanford University, USA, tested the willpower of a group of four-year-olds in the following experiment. Mischel and his colleagues presented the four-year-olds with a plate of treats such as marshmallows, saying that the researcher had to go out of the room for a few minutes. Each child was then given a simple choice: if s/he waited until the researcher returned, s/he could have two marshmallows. If s/he simply couldn't wait, s/he could ring a bell and the researcher would come back immediately, but s/he would only be allowed one marshmallow.

The researchers discovered that those who were able to delay gratification at four years of age were more successful in later life because they had learned the life skill of developing their willpower to succeed in overcoming difficult tasks on the way to achieving their goals.[1]

My mother's game was something similar and I loved it. Every day I couldn't wait to put more pebbles in the box. I thought up loads of challenges and then ran through them with relish. I didn't eat that bar of chocolate I so wanted. I ran errands when I didn't want to. I helped around the house. I did anything that was a challenge for me just to win at the game of filling up the box with those little stones. I discovered in myself an intrinsic motivation to win

---

1 H. N. Mischel and W. Mischel, 'The Development of Children's Knowledge of Self-control Strategies', in *Child Development* 54, 1983, pp. 603–19.

and to reap the reward of my mother's joy at recognising my achievement. By focusing on challenges and difficulties in this positive way, my mother was teaching me the value of being able to turn a negative or challenging situation into a good experience that produces positive actions.

Perhaps it is good to pause here and relate this thinking to the business organisations we work in today and to focus on the reason why 'intrinsic motivation' is thought to be one of the most essential components of a successful company.[2] Where workers are intrinsically motivated to overcome challenges, and more importantly when they are recognised publicly by their immediate superiors for a job well done, businesses flourish.

To return to my childhood story, not only was this game of 'filling the box with stones' a good way of training my willpower to be a strong and flexible muscle for future challenges, it also showed me that I thrived on challenge. I learned that if I focused on a challenge in a certain way, as a game, I could win and enjoy winning, instead of becoming depressed over difficulties, and that problems could be overcome and not be overwhelming.

I realised that another important lesson of Focus is:

---

2 T. Amabile, 'How to Kill Creativity', *Harvard Business Review*, September 1998, pp. 77–87.

it is not enough to know *what* you need to focus on to be successful, it is even more important to understand *how* you focus and how the way you focus can be very beneficial.

Focus is Forever

I have never forgotten these lessons from my mother. She died one year later, when I was eight years old, but thanks to being wrapped in the strength of a loving and giving father, I was able to sustain my interest in developing the skills of Clear Thinking and Focus to achieve success for both myself and others.

Over twenty-five years later, while studying for a PhD in philosophy, I created many of the techniques in this book. I now wish to offer these to you in a way and style that will make it easy to recognise your own innate abilities – perhaps learned from your parents or grandparents also – so that you can articulate them to achieve what it is you strive for at this point in your life.

Having Clear Focus means being able to think clearly from our desires to our decisions. But first we need to be able to answer the question: why do we find it so hard to focus?

2

WHY DO WE FIND IT SO HARD TO FOCUS?

While born with the strong ability to focus clearly on what we need to survive as infants, very often as adults we find it difficult to know what to focus on in our lives and how to focus. Furthermore, even when we desperately want to achieve something, we often lose the focus that is so necessary for our success.

Why do we find it so hard to retain clear direction in what we do? We can all see that our fears and inability to work with difficulties can pull us down and outweigh our commitment to succeed. But do you notice that you can sometimes give up on what you want because, perhaps, you simply believe you can't get it? Or you might just tell yourself that you don't really want to achieve your goal. So belief and genuine need are two qualities which are necessary to help us remain focused on what we want.

I am going to concentrate on the kind of Clear-Thinking skills that we need to achieve Focus and I am going to take it for granted that you will bring these two qualities of your personal belief and genuine need to succeed to sustain your Focus as you read. That doesn't mean that you have to achieve everything you want right now, or that you have to read this book in one sitting. I hope you will be able to dip in and out of it when you require a little refocus and that it will be the right tonic for you when you need to get back on the road again, as well as being the type of reading material that will also allow you to rest a little in between tasks.

I am assuming that if you are reading this book you really want to focus on achieving your ambitions and you believe in your abilities to succeed (most of the time anyway!). I will assume that as we work through the thinking techniques, there may be distractions as well as illuminations. I hope you will discover that there are easy, accessible ways to tap into your ability to think clearly and effectively.

Just a few words also on your environment: the situation into which you bring your Focus to get the best result. When trying to make clear decisions years ago, the mantra around the difficulties people encountered in focusing on what to do was always 'we don't have enough information'. 'We don't know what to focus on,' they would say, 'because we cannot see the full picture and, therefore, might be making bad decisions.' This is no longer true for the modern world, in which the greater problem is 'information overload' and our inability to critically evaluate it all. To make matters worse the world seems to have become addicted to the idea that we never have enough data in the moment. Added to this is the temptation to google everything in order to find more information, as if having further information from an 'authoritative' source somehow gives us the knowledge to make a decision.

The result of information overload and the inability to distinguish knowledge from information can often paralyse us until there is a crisis which forces us to make a decision. So we fall into 'crisis management' mode, solving the symptoms but not the cause of our problems: indeed we may not even recognise the true problems or issues, nor, as a result, the best decision to make.

I am reminded of the words of T. S. Eliot: 'Where is the wisdom we have lost in knowledge? Where is the knowledge we have lost in information?'[3] He also asked, 'Where is the life we have lost in living?' Sobering thoughts indeed, and hopefully they demonstrate the importance of Clear Thinking and how you need to be focused to live a satisfying life.

Remember, your desires, needs or deepest wishes will give you the urgency to focus. They will tell you what to focus on – and with that knowledge we can build on your skills of *how* to focus in order to succeed.

There has been much recent research on the functions

---

3 T. S. Eliot, *The Rock* (Faber, 1934).

of the brain. Neuroscientists have identified what parts of the brain we use when we think and cognitive scientists have explored cognitive illusions and 'thinking errors'. This helps us to be more aware of how we think and how to improve the way we do so, and there are many reference books you can consult to find out more on the theoretical aspects of how the mind works. My aim is to provide a practical guidebook on how to develop strong Focus, so that you can feel confident in your actions. I will bring you from Focus to Action in a very simple way, based on a wide knowledge of ancient philosophy as well as the practical wisdom of our parents and grandparents.

When I was a student of philosophy, both as an undergraduate and a postgraduate in two different universities in two countries, my interest in how we think – how we use our reasoning processes to convince ourselves we are right (or wrong) – was very focused and included the study of early philosophers such as Aristotle and Plato. With this background, I created the first 'Clear & Critical Thinking' training module over twenty years ago and since then I have worked with international corporations and organisations, designing and developing programmes on improving thinking skills for successful leadership, problem-solving and decision-making. The ideas in this book build on those in my first book *Quick Thinking On Your Feet*, where I looked at the art of manipulation and how to remain focused without losing your train of thought when, all around, others are losing theirs – in other words: how to remain cool in hot situations.[4]

Included in this book are the stories of ordinary people in some extraordinary and interesting situations. All of these people have one thing in common – they have used their incredible Focus to turn a difficult situation into a resounding success.

Whatever your aim, I hope that this book will help you to achieve the concentration and determination to attain what you want, how you want it and when you want it.

---

4   Valerie Pierce, *Quick Thinking On Your Feet* (Mercier Press, 2003).

3

A Simple Model for Success

Great thinking needs great actions to achieve effective and sustainable solutions. This book is a guide to Clear Thinking in Action – the art of being in control of what you want, when you want it. It is a matter of taking simple steps to achieve success, at your own pace and in your own time.

The idea is that you can take graded steps, according to your own desire, need and ability, to become a clear thinker. We don't all need to be expert thinkers all of the time. Sometimes we need just a little bit of Clear Thinking to help us on our way, and at other times we need to be much more qualified in what we do. This book will help you to dip into the grade and ability you require. That way you can clarify what you wish to do by breaking your goals into simple, easy-to-manage parts. You can also rest on these 'steps', to take stock and give yourself a little reward as you progress that bit further. For this reason, I am choosing the metaphor and visual of a spiral staircase to help you crystallise your progress as you develop. I would like you to imagine climbing this staircase, determined to reach your ultimate goal. With the visual of a stairway you can see that you are progressing on a continuous path towards your unique Peak Performance.

Another reason to use this visual is because of the French expression, *esprit de l'escalier* or 'staircase wit', which refers to what happens when we are *not able* to focus. Have you ever had that awful feeling when you come out of a meeting where you lost focus and are angry because you didn't do or say what you had intended? Then, annoyingly, hours later, you know in detail what you should have said?

This ability to focus too late, usually as we are going up the stairs to bed (hence the expression 'staircase wit'), is infuriating, but at the same time shows us that we do know how to get what we want, but somehow lose that capability 'in the moment' or at the time we need it so badly. It is amazing how our brains can click back into gear and tell us exactly what we should have done when it is too late.

I wish to bring that staircase knowledge right into the present moment so that you can learn to work through its details, ready for when you need it. As you become familiar with your personal steps in your development, you will be able to call on that 'staircase wit' before it's too late.

You can see the structure for the pathway to successful action in the spiral staircase in Figure 1. 'Focus' is the backbone (the pole in the centre of the staircase), just as it is the basis of your ability to succeed. The steps of

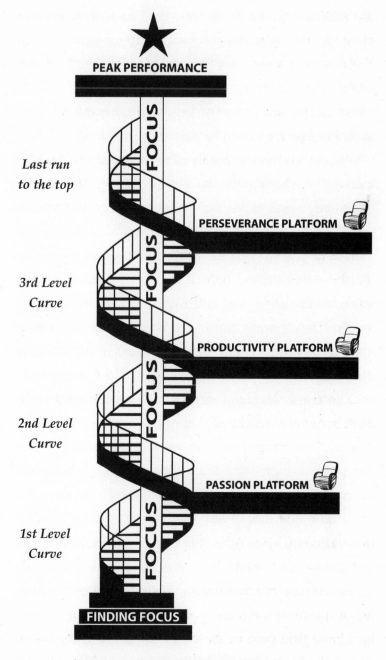

Figure 1: The Spiral Staircase of Success

23

the staircase then wind around the Focus of the pole, as they are the steps that you will climb up to reach your full potential, your Peak Performance. The platforms on your staircase are places where you can rest, put down your reading and reflect on how you can implement the learning and ideas you have just digested.

We all know the much-used expression 'learning curve', i.e. the experience we go through to acquire knowledge and expertise. So, most importantly, there are three learning curves to your spiral staircase that will help you to gain the skills you need to secure the Focus of that central pole. As you climb the steps and make your turns, you will experience these 'learning curves' as separate entities of development that help you to advance, champion and take control of your thinking.

The three 'learning curves' or development skills that help you to achieve your goals are:

- ❖ Passion
- ❖ Productivity
- ❖ Perseverance.

Another reason for using the visual of a spiral staircase with its resting platforms and learning curves is to carry you upwards towards your Peak Performance in a way that ensures your thinking cannot spiral downwards. Many of us worry about the direction of our thinking when we find ourselves in a panic or a difficult situation, so my aim is to give you a place of safety in this book where you can take stock of what you need to do in order to be in control of your desired outcomes.

The different sections of this book will explain these learning curves in detail, but first I wish to give you a short understanding of the power that each skill has to carry you up the staircase to success.

Your Personal Learning Curves

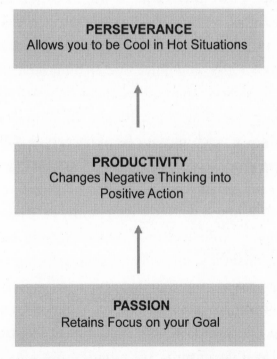

Figure 2: Your Personal Learning Curves. Starting with self-awareness, these three critical building blocks develop the required tools for Clear Thinking to achieve confident and creative actions.

PASSION

We put 'A' at the beginning of much that we do. For example, A is the first letter of our alphabet and it is often used as the symbol for the first thing we have to do at the top of a list of priorities – a, b, c, etc. In addition, 'A' is what students wish to achieve in their exams as an illustration of excellence. So with 'A' we learn to put first things first while at the same time reaching for excellence.

A is also the first letter of the word 'act' – your ultimate goal when you focus. For your Focus to be successful you must concentrate on some action you wish to achieve and have the stamina and staying power to realise it. So as a reminder of how to remain focused I am using the acronym 'ACT' to illustrate the actions in each of your learning curves. 'A' is the reminder that to achieve successful actions you must begin your journey by 'Advancing'. As you progress you will follow A with 'C', your ability to 'Champion' your cause. And finally, 'T' is your ability to 'Take Control' of both yourself and others to reach your ultimate goals.

So, starting with A as the symbol for your first step on the stairs to Clear-Thinking excellence, with *Passion* you flex your Focus muscles to A – Advance. Before you can act you need to be able to gain the courage to stand up and get moving, and also, before you can think clearly, you need to know what you want to think clearly about. Being *passionate* develops your curiosity and feelings of enthusiasm about having a goal and being able to focus clearly enough to reach it.

For example, in order to have successful discussions at work you need to retain focus so as to concentrate under pressure. I call this being able to advance, as opposed to standing still, being diverted onto the wrong track or simply losing the plot. (And it's not always others who manipulate our thinking to go off track – we are also experts at going 'all over the place' when we should be focused on one thing only.) With Passion we are able to focus in such a way that we remain on track to reach our goals. In Chapter 5 I will show you how to think with Passion – how to focus on goals and not get caught up in ego identity or manipulation, which can do so much to muddle Clear Thinking. You will learn to understand the difference between your 'passions' and your 'emotions', and how they can work for you and not against you.

A note about your feelings as your foundation for growth

Your feelings of attachment to your goal comprise your strongest and most powerful ally to help you to remain focused. It is the amount of feeling you have for your objective which will be the deciding factor on whether you succeed or fail. This is my basic and most fundamental premise for you to remember in taking your first steps to achieving what you want.

My belief is different from the more traditional view that to control your feelings when striving to achieve goals, you must detach from them and think in a logical, abstract manner. We are often led to believe that to achieve we must think in a very logical, linear way. Distinctions are made in thinking, such as logic, emotion, imagination and intuition, and we are told that the two opposites in these elements are logic and emotion. These are seen as contradictory ways of thinking and are often understood as logic *versus* emotion. It is often claimed that if we are emotional, we cannot be logical and, by implication, cannot make decisions that are good for us, as we will not be able to distinguish between the facts as they are and as we think they are. We are often advised that emotion clouds judgement as prejudices, fears and biases give a distorted view of reality, which in many cases is not to our advantage.

In fact many organisations run their meetings in this manner and participants are told to leave their emotions outside the room and to think in a logical step-by-step process so as to reach satisfactory solutions. Cold abstract logic is thus set against warm and fuzzy feelings and thought to be far superior by some, although greatly lacking by others. Countless arguments then ensue about which way of making decisions or achieving goals is better. I believe this is futile and that neither of these ways is better since there is a deep flaw in this contradictory labelling and deconstructive way of thinking.

I want to counter this theory and to show you that your feelings are essential to achieving your goals, so it is vital not to repress them and give your thinking over to abstract logic.

What is fundamental for success is that you become aware of how to focus your feelings. Being aware of how you focus your feelings, where you are attaching them and what they are attached to, will ensure you can achieve your goals in a way that is far more efficient than by any piece of logical analysis. It is by using your feelings in a different way, a way in which they are in full control, that you will be able to achieve the result you want.

I will show you how to be aware of where your feelings are focused, because your feelings, the 'soul' of your energy pool, can propel you into 'heaven' or 'hell'. It is in knowing *how* to focus them that will decide where you end up.

Top Tip for First Learning Curve – Passion:
Choose a goal and then stick with it through thick and thin

PRODUCTIVITY

Passion feels exciting, but of course there is no use being passionate if we cannot do anything. How many people are very passionate about what they want but are still sitting around talking about it? And to whomever will listen?

Passion alone is not enough: it is simply the first step to maintaining Focus and the art of Clear Thinking. Passion would be useless without the 'next step' of *Productivity*, which is your ability to produce a viable action that will help your dreams become a reality. Without Productivity you would remain in the sphere of wishful thinking.

The second learning curve on the spiral staircase is the development of Productivity – the ability to think in a productive way to achieve your goal. Productivity is the ability to turn passionate beliefs into action because productive thinking is about getting things done – it champions the individual's desires and abilities to achieve his/her goals.

Our lives are made up of relatively random acts involving what we desire, are interested in or want to be part of. This may sound like a very depressing statement, but I highlight it to focus attention on the fact that it is you, and only you, who give meaning and value to your life. Our random acts become important according to the amount of love, desire or need we feel for them. Before you can think clearly about that promotion at work, ask yourself if you really want it. Do you really want that job you are after? Do you really want to change career? Because if you don't, no amount of Clear Thinking will get it for you.

If you suffer from low self-esteem or self-belief, you will simply sabotage your ability to get what you want. If you don't really want something or feel you don't deserve it or indeed can't be bothered, your thoughts will be counter-productive and you will end up with a self-fulfilling prophecy of 'I knew I would never be able to get that job' or 'I knew that job was already someone else's, even before I applied for it'. This is simply an assumption you make with no evidence, when you don't get what you want.

One way to overcome these negative tendencies is to be kind to ourselves and to establish positive meanings around our desires and abilities to achieve. First of all, you need to be clear about your goal but, most importantly for your second step in Clear Thinking, you have to be aware of the type of meaning you are putting onto your ability to achieve it. Because we create our own meanings that help us achieve our actions, it is up to you to make them positive, not negative – I believe the choice is yours.

For example, I know as I write that my purpose is to create a successful book which I hope the reader will enjoy and find useful. The meaning that I give to my purpose, how I understand it, helps me to either keep my focus or lose it. If I believe that writing this book is going to be an extremely difficult task, that I may fall at the first hurdle and indeed not be able to achieve my goal, then it is going to be very hard to keep myself focused and motivated. If, on the contrary, I am excited by this project, I understand that although it is a challenge I know I will step up to the mark and enjoy it – this positive meaning helps me to keep my focus even through the most exacting moments. We have a choice about how we understand ourselves and what we choose to focus on. And I believe it is more intelligent to be kind to, and not hard on, ourselves as we progress.

Developing your skill of Productivity or productive thinking is to champion your desires and abilities. As you already know, your Passion to reach your goal gives you the connection to that goal that will keep you focused on achieving it. To feel passionate about what you want gives you that purpose and self-belief that is so important to success. Your next step of championing your goals will help you to focus on the meaning you are giving to what you want. By focusing on your productive thinking abilities you will become aware of how connected you really are to your goal, and it will become apparent whether you are brave, strong and innovative enough to transform any negative thinking you have into positive action to help you on your way.

Productivity requires you to be a champion of your cause in order to think clearly to achieve it. We will look in detail in Chapter 6 at how to do this, but let me end this introduction by giving you a marvellous example about how being positive and productive through a difficult or challenging situation can produce stunning success. This story was told to me by a member of staff at one of my favourite clients, one of the best-loved museums in Europe, and concerns a very successful exhibition they ran in 2013. This story has many components that you will like – glamour, passion, pain and ultimate success.

I have been working with this client for over twelve years, teaching Clear & Critical Thinking skills for Effective Influencing. One very popular method we utilise is a thinking technique that I have devised, which uses the power of stressful or fearful thinking to create positive actions and outcomes. This technique, which I call the DNA method, is a way of turning negative thinking into positive action. It means achieving your Dream (D) by working on your Negatives (N) to produce a desired positive Action (A). The following story is an example of extraordinary success gained by using this very simple DNA thinking tool.

It was reluctantly decided in 2012 that it would no longer be viable to keep a small and very specialised satellite museum open to the public. Though well located in a popular area in the Arts Quarter of London, which also includes the Royal Opera House as well as the nearby West End theatres, the museum itself was in a difficult-to-reach location, within a myriad of small streets. It had been an archive of special artists and their artefacts in the entertainment industry, but was now seen as only serving a niche market of specialists. It was additionally very costly to run and was losing a substantial amount of money. It seemed that the logical conclusion was to close it and solve the problems as shown below:

Problems of the Specialist Museum

- **Location – too small**
- **Niche Celebrity Status**
- **Losing Profits**

= **Close down Museum**

Figure 3: The Museum Story

In fact that is how most people would think. When we focus on problems as if they are 'reasons' to stop the process of achieving our goals, then with that kind of focus and logic it does make sense to give up. We often see this happen at company meetings, or, if we are honest, we can notice we do this ourselves. That is, we 'rationalise' our problems as reasons why we cannot achieve what we want.

However, with Clear Focus and quality thinking when we champion our goals, we can use these very same reasons as markers of information on how to solve our problems and so reach our goals. That is, we can change a 'No, because' into a 'Yes, if'. And that is what the museum did. They took the three negative issues – Bad Location, Niche Celebrity Status and Loss of Profits – and were then able to focus on what they needed to work on and to change in order to succeed. And so they did, and in the process created one of the most successful exhibitions of all time.

The first problem: Location was too small.

Solution: they found a much bigger area within the main museum building itself, not far away. They also created a virtual museum to ensure the location could easily expand. This way of dealing imaginatively with a 'location' problem ensured that this specialised theatre museum was not shut down. It is still open to the public and all staff jobs are secure.

The second problem: Niche Celebrity Status.

Solution: in 2013 they created one of the most successful exhibitions of all time in this specialist museum by exhibiting the works and personal effects of a celebrity who had worldwide recognition and iconic status, thus drawing in a huge audience.

The third problem: the museum was losing money.

Solution: they made this 2013 exhibition fee-paying. On the first night ticket sales reached the thousands. By mid-June they had sold over half a million tickets and the numbers continued to rise. The result is that this exhibition not only paid for the upkeep of the newly located specialist museum but also now helps with much-needed funds for other parts of the museum.

As you can see from the graphic below, using negative thinking, focused in this way, allows you to reach extraordinary success.

How Negative Thinking delivers Successful Actions

Bad location = Find a new one: real & virtual

Niche Celebrity Status = Find a worldwide attraction

Losing Profits = Gaining profits by carrying out 1 & 2 above

= Saving Specialist Museum in a creative and exciting way

Figure 4: Steps to Getting Things Done

Top Tip for Second Learning Curve – Productivity:
Negative thinking does not always lead to negative feelings or negativity
Negative thinking is one of the most powerful thinking tools to produce positive, innovative actions

Perseverance

Perseverance is the backbone and stamina of Focus on the final steps to success. Your last curve on the staircase towards achieving your full potential through Clear Thinking is the ability to take control of how you communicate your thoughts in order to get things done. Up to now, your first two 'learning curves' have concentrated on the need to 'Focus to Act' to advance and champion your cause. For these last steps we need to reverse that idea, as success is now dependent on how you act to keep both yourself and others focused. We no longer 'Focus to Act', now we need to 'Act with Focus'.

This reversal – Act with Focus – is essential if you are not to get lost in action, perhaps never to be found. These last steps require Perseverance and a greater need to remain focused. This highest grade of Focus and Clear Thinking is required for navigating your way through difficult meetings and negotiations, so as to get what you want, when you want it.

These steps on the staircase are the highest and the most difficult. Visually, you can see it is not easy, as it is at these dizzy heights of achievement that most of us can get vertigo and lose sight of what we want to achieve. As you reach for your goal you may feel it was easier when you started out on your journey.

The final steps through 'Perseverance' are more

difficult, but they ensure you can take control as you go through the quagmire of group decision-making. You need to be able to deal with situations when the opinions of yourself and others fall prey to certain thinking errors, allowing you to fall at this last hurdle on the road to transforming ideas into action.

You need to be able to act in a way that never loses focus, no matter how much information overload bombards you, no matter how much resistance confronts you and no matter how much you doubt yourself. The learning curve of 'Perseverance' helps to change conflict into peaceful collaboration and shaky actions into committed decisions.

It is so easy to get distracted. However, to Act with Focus ensures you won't and it is my aim here to show you the techniques of resilience and motivation to achieve Clear Thinking when you need it at this advanced level and stage of 'Quick Thinking on your feet'.

Let me tell you the story of a course participant who carried this out to great effect. She was able to spot the thinking error of her garage mechanic, who was not able to see that just because one act precedes another it does not mean that the first act causes the second one. With Anne's Clear Thinking she was able to see this and in the process saved herself a substantial amount of money.

Anne sent me this email after we had worked together on one of my training courses. I was delighted to receive a wonderful example of how Clear Thinking can be achieved, and can achieve so much.

I am the unfortunate owner of a car bought four years ago from new. I have had so many problems in that time with the electrics of this thing that I was beginning to wonder if I was driving a mobile disco. The dashboard lights seemed to come on and go off in time to the music that I was playing on the CDs ... This particular day I took it to the dealer to complain (again) as this time it really needed to be fixed as the car was due its first NCT and would not pass with this problem. It was supposed to have been sorted out twelve months previously.

While the car was in the garage the manager rang me to come and see him about a problem, so off I went ... only for him to attack me when I arrived about the state of the bodywork of the car. My car had been involved in a crash, and was repaired by an authorised panel-beater by the way ... He said that the problem I now had with the car was caused by the repairs where an essential grommet was missing and that it was not his fault.

This problem now meant that I would have to pay €1,100 to repair my car to pass the NCT. Normally this would have sent me into a rage and I would rant on and on … but I stopped for a couple of moments and then told him that what he was saying might not in fact be true. He was only in the realms of supposing and supposition … This took him by surprise and he asked me to explain …

I explained that the problem involved the chaffing of wires. He said this had begun because of my car body repair work six months previously. But how did he know this problem may have started then – it could have started twelve months ago when his garage had my car in for repair of the 'mobile disco' problem. Or it could even have happened eighteen months previously, when the garage again had the car for a while, or indeed the problem could have been there four years ago, when I first bought the car.

Also, their service people had the car in for a full service three weeks ago, which involved taking wheels off, where, by the way, the grommet was missing, so it was possible to suppose that they removed it and never replaced it. I explained that if he could suppose that the grommet was missing as a result of the bodywork repairs, then I could suppose that it had never been there, or that it went missing on one of the occasions when the car was with them for repair.

He stayed silent for several minutes. 'Leave it with me,' he said, 'and I'll come back to you with a decision.'

The next day he called me to say that he had changed his mind. He could not justify a charge for new ABS components that were damaged through the wire chaffing, which in total was €1,100, as neither he nor I could prove when this happened. And he apologised to me for charging into an attack to blame someone else for a problem which may have been on-going for four years ... Without stopping for those moments and thinking, I would most likely have made matters worse by letting fly at him and most likely have ended up being thrown out of the garage along with my glorious heap of a car.

Anne's last comments to me were:

Thank you for showing me how to think on my feet in this type of situation. I surprised myself with how calm and collected I was instead of firing away without thinking first.

What a lovely story of success! It is my wish that you will have similar stories of achievement when you finish reading this book.

My wish is that whatever steps of the Focus staircase you decide to step onto or stay on, this book will create a safe space for you to achieve your dreams and goals, whatever they are.

Top Tip for Third Learning Curve – Perseverance:
Make sure you understand the difference between good logic and bad reasons

I hope you enjoyed these short introductions to your three learning curves and are looking forward to working with them in depth later on. For now we need to talk a little about how you find Focus and take your first steps to success.

Part 2:

Applying the Model

Figure 5: True Understanding

4

YOUR FIRST STEPS

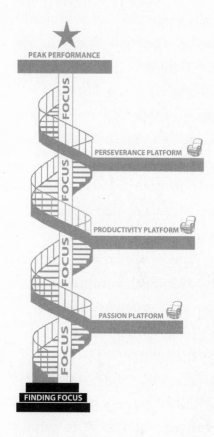

FINDING FOCUS: HOW TO FIND THE RIGHT FOCUS

Before you can step onto your stairway you need to ensure that you are focusing on the correct goal. To climb your intended steps you need to take some time out to make sure you understand your purpose.

As you step onto the spiral staircase, and while you are sitting comfortably on your first steps contemplating what you would like to focus on, I will begin by taking you through some simple techniques to ensure that when you focus on a subject, topic or problem, you can be confident that you are focusing on the correct or right one.

Finding what you really want to focus on will then allow you to continue with confidence up the steps of the staircase so that with your Passion, Productivity and Perseverance you can ACT, i.e. Advance your goal, Champion its delivery and Take Control of your environment, to ensure that your goals become a reality (see Chapter 7).

Clear Focus needs true understanding: to work towards your ideal, you need to both understand and recognise your problem situation.

(A) Understanding

One of the most common difficulties in Clear Thinking is being able to identify and focus on the real problem or opportunity you wish to pursue. Identifying the problem means being able to understand it as well as to recognise if there is a problem.

Most of the literature on this subject concentrates on being able to recognise the problem, so I will look at that in more detail in a moment. But before you begin to expend your energy and focus on a particular issue, it is best to understand the problem and be sure that there is one. Let me give you a short example.

Two men played five games of chess. Each won three games. How did that happen?

Try to answer this question for a moment. Are you puzzled and do you find it difficult to find an answer? People often think there is a problem here because they understand that these two men are playing against each other. But of course if they are playing other people, then there is no problem. We only think there is a problem because of the way we understand the situation.

Before you focus on tackling a problem it is a good idea to check if it is your understanding of the situation that is perhaps creating the problem. What an easy way to solve problems!

(B) RECOGNISING THE PROBLEM OR OPPORTUNITY

Proper recognition of a problem or opportunity can be difficult to achieve for two reasons:

1   Our thinking is blinkered (over-focused) so we cannot see the bigger picture.
2   Our thinking is so vague (under-focused) that we cannot see the core issue.

Let's look at the first reason – being blinkered. Each of us suffers from what is called the 'confirmation bias', which means that we will always search for what we already know or believe. If we believe that we are looking at a marketing problem or an operational issue or opportunity, then that is what we will find: a marketing problem or an operational issue or opportunity.

A lovely story to illustrate this phenomenon of the confirmation bias is the famous eighteenth-century philosophical problem called the 'Black Swan', where people believed all swans were white because they continually saw white swans. And each time they saw another white swan it confirmed that all swans were indeed white. Even when they saw a black swan they would simply conclude that it wasn't a swan – until they had irrefutable evidence that, yes, these black things that looked like black swans were indeed black swans. And so they eventually had to change their beliefs.

Because it is so hard to change our beliefs, we tend to confirm them wherever we go, even when in search of something new. This can make it difficult to identify genuine problems or see new opportunities.

The second reason – being vague in our thinking – is just as problematic. It is a serious flaw that can blind us to the core issue(s) of a problem or opportunity. Our error is that we can *only* see 'the big picture'. That is, we are so dazzled by the wonderful vision we have set our sights on that we are completely unaware of the complex steps or actions we need to take to achieve it. So, as we progress towards our goal we will tend to fall at the first hurdle. We will find ourselves saying, 'I never thought this involved so much or would be so hard to achieve' or 'I never thought this would cost so much money' or 'I was never told about the many aspects of this situation I needed to consider', etc.

These are real difficulties when it comes to Clear Focus – for how can we know what to focus on? How do we know how to prioritise?

A great deal of training and self-help literature tells us 'how to prioritise' – to make lists of what to do and then to tackle these items one by one. But the assumption is that you already know what your priorities are! My big question is still: how do I know what to put at the top of my list, i.e. how do I know what to focus on first? I don't want to be like poor Joe who focuses on one aspect of his business at the cost of another (see page 66). We need to know what is essential to our success. How can we cut through all the noise of information overload and the chatter and opinions of others, to arrive at our ultimate Focus?

To have Clear Focus we need to be able to see the bigger picture and all of its aspects

To create a better vision of all the possibilities in problem-solving and opportunity assessments, we need to be able to see all the items on our list without making a prejudgement about where they are positioned. We need to be able to see the big picture of our environment so that we can make a conscious choice of what we need to focus on to get us started – to advance.

There is a Clear-Thinking technique that I particularly like and which helps me to define my Focus by being able to look at all aspects of my situation before deciding what to prioritise. This technique is called 'The Clock'.

As you can see, this very simple, easy technique forces us to see at least twelve aspects of a problem situation before we can say that we can 'identify the real problem' or 'assess the real opportunity'. Once we can see so many aspects of a situation it is then easier to have the confidence to know that we have seen the full picture and go on to choose what to focus on to build success.

Development activity: 'The Clock'

Think of a goal you want to achieve or a problem you want to solve. On a blank sheet of paper, write this objective in the centre of the page and circle it. To make sure you have included everything in your environment that can be of help to you in achieving your goal, draw at least twelve aspects you need to consider in a clock-like fashion around this goal. This will help you focus on what you need to do to advance. If you find you have more than twelve aspects, you can use the twenty-four-hour clock – and many organisations that I work with do. Now look at your clock and ask yourself some challenging questions:

- ❖ What is the best way to focus here?

- ❖ Which one of these aspects do I want to focus on as my top priority?

- ❖ Am I focusing on the right issue?

- ❖ Are there other issues/ways of solving my problem that I had not noticed before?

- ❖ Can I shift my focus and concentrate on something else on this clock in order to reach my goal?

The idea is that by looking clearly at all aspects of your situation you can now choose a focus that you are sure and confident is the right step to achieve your goal.

What follows is a story from a lady who did just that.

CASE HISTORY: JULIE, THE TRAINING PROFESSIONAL

On starting out on my career as a training professional, I had a huge fear of talking to large groups. This, of course, was a very bad situation for me. As a trainer my job is to be an excellent public speaker and to captivate an audience in the 'palm of my hands', sometimes for hours at a time.

My fears were very strong and terribly frightening, and not without some real substance. As a child growing up I suffered from a very bad stammer and only recently had begun to speak fluently in normal situations with family and friends. Once I became nervous again, however, the stutter would return, and fear sometimes made me speechless. I would think to myself 'if you talk to a large group, you will stammer', or 'if you talk to a large group you will forget what you want to say', or even worse 'if you talk to a large group your voice will go'.

My focus was utterly on my fear of public speaking, even though this was feeding my fears and so making them even stronger.

How could I overcome this situation? It needed a big step, but what could I do? Then I thought to myself, 'since focusing on my fear of public speaking is actually very successful, in that it is making me speechless, perhaps a different focus on another risk or higher desire might be just as powerful and make me reach my goal this time – to speak fluently'.

My idea was to change my focus and play to a higher risk or desire, a desire that is so strong it might make me forget my fear of public speaking. And I found it. For me the greater fear or risk was the awful situation of looking irrational or foolish in front of my clients, while attempting to build a strong professional reputation with them.

So I rang up a list of companies, introducing myself and my product. When they became interested and said they would like to know more, I suggested the best method would be if I could give a short presentation to a large number of their managers. This appealed to them as it was also very cost effective for them. So I made an appointment to give a presentation within the month. That way I had time to prepare and psych myself up, so I could feel confident with the knowledge that I had.

However, the most important motivator for me was that backing out now was not a possibility as my reputation was far dearer to me than my fear of speaking in public. Having set myself up to meet a higher goal more precious to me than my fear of public speaking, I now had shifted my focus from my fear of public speaking to my need and desire to follow through on my promises. So I had to go through with it. And it worked! Changing my focus changed my ability to succeed.

Slowly but surely, I got used to giving lots of presentations and can now do so without a moment's hesitation, stammer free – and now I actually enjoy them.

People create success by using Clear Personal Focus

I hope you enjoyed Julie's story. What I really like about it is the clear illustration of how changing our Focus can change our ability to succeed. That is why I particularly like the exercise of 'The Clock' and how it allows us to choose what is important over what is not before we begin to focus and prioritise. This ensures that you can focus on what really matters.

The clock is also a timepiece, which is a good reminder for us all that we need time to focus and to decide what is most important to us before we start on our own personal road to Action.

Focus is a kind of backbone, the centre of our existence, and it will be important for you to find your backbone – your special strength that no one can ever take from you. To end this chapter on finding Focus, therefore, I thought you might like to read the following inspiring little story:

The Music

Once upon a time there lived a famous musician. He was so famous that no festival could ever take place in the kingdom without his most beautiful harp playing. For a festival to be worthy of that name, Mr Figueredo had to be there, playing his beautiful music to lift the hearts and move the bodies of all attending.

One evening as Mr Figueredo was returning from a wedding, thieves set upon him.

As he gently sauntered along a lonely road with his two mules, one mule carrying his beautiful harp and the other mule carrying Mr Figueredo, thieves attacked him, taking all his goods and leaving him badly hurt.

The next morning he was found by a passer-by. He had been badly beaten and looked like he was nearer to death than to life. With what was left of his voice he said, 'They took the mules …

'They took the harp …'

'But,' he continued with a smile, 'they couldn't take the music …'[5]

QUESTIONS FOR YOU

What is your passion that is worth more than anything else and that no one can take from you? For Mr Figueredo it was his music, for others it is art, books, love, sports, freedom or the simple joy of being alive.

What is your secret flame that no one can take from you and which will always keep you happy?

What is your strength that you will always have no matter how difficult it might be to reach your goal or create your business/ideas?

Please note your special strength below before you step onto your staircase to succeed and before you

---

5   Eduardo Galeano, *Sens dessus dessous* (Homnisphères, Paris, 2004); translated by Valerie Pierce.

begin to work through the learning curves needed to reach the top. To be aware of your special strength will help you to remain focused as you strive to achieve your goal.

YOUR STORY – YOUR STRENGTH

_____

_____

_____

_____

_____

_____

_____

_____

_____

_____

_____

_____

_____

Your First Learning Curve: Passion

Once you have found your Focus, your first learning curve is knowing how to ensure that your feelings and desires work for you, not against you, when you reach for your goals. For example, are you excited about achieving your goal or do you see it with trepidation and wish you'd never got up this morning? And more importantly, what effect do you think these feelings have on your ability to achieve? For example, do you notice that when you are excited about your projects you are able to think of lots of new and exciting ideas? Or the opposite, do you notice that, if you hate your project, trying to think about it is like looking into a black hole?

Real success requires a determination and focus that keeps us glued to our goals. That is because it is so easy to get distracted with the information overload and the myriad of options we meet along the way. So, how can you ensure that you will remain consistently directed towards what you want to achieve?

I'd like you to sit down on the first curve of your staircase while I tell you of a skill, a distinction in Clear Thinking, that will stabilise your Focus at the start, during and at the end of your journey to reach your goals.

USE YOUR PASSIONS TO CONTROL YOUR EMOTIONS

This distinction is very simple. It is between being passionate or being emotional. If you are clear about whether you are passionate or emotional about what you want to achieve, you will be able to focus in a way that matters – because one leads to success, the other to failure.

Let me explain what I mean by these two defini-
tions. When we are passionate about our projects, our
feelings are attached to the projects themselves with
the result that we have a lot more strength to reach
the end point.

For example, let's pretend you have a pet project
at work. You have worked incredibly hard, finding all
the evidence to back up the likely success of your idea
and you have created a strong PowerPoint presentation to run past your colleagues at your next meeting.
If you are passionate about your project you will have
thought of many ways to withstand any criticisms and
overcome any obstacles. Indeed you may be delighted
to have questions and difficulties thrown at you
because you see this as a way of opening your mind to
achieve even greater success.

Being passionate means that every thought you
have is understood as a way of getting closer to your
goal. You will never think: 'Will I be able to do this?';
a person who is passionate about achieving their goals
will always go straight to: 'How do I achieve this?'

Passion creates energy in our thinking. Passion
motivates us to create ideas and solutions we would
normally never even imagine because passion propels
us to move closer to our goals, through stronger and
greater thinking skills and abilities.

When you go into that meeting and someone criticises what you are doing, it's okay – because you

are passionate, you will have thoughts like: 'That's interesting, there is a problem here I hadn't thought of. I am so glad this person has brought up this issue now, so early on in the thinking process, as it means we can fix this problem and have a stronger goal.' In other words, all your thinking skills are firmly connected to achieving the goal you wish to reach, working for you and not against you.

Being emotional is completely different. Some people who are emotional will never admit it and perhaps not even be aware of it. Emotional people often say things like 'I'm really passionate about this project' but you know by their behaviour and responses that they are not passionate: in fact they are very emotional.

To explain this difference: imagine again that you are very connected to your project. You have worked hard on it, as above, but this time you are emotional and not passionate about it. Being emotional means that instead of your thoughts and feelings being connected to your project, they are connected to your 'ego' – your ability to do your project. If we take the same scenario where you are giving a PowerPoint presentation of your work to your colleagues and someone criticises you, this time, being emotional, you will not think: 'I'm glad they brought up this problem early on so that I can fix it.' Now, being emotional, you will have thoughts like: 'I knew the minute I mentioned any new ideas, *she* would start; I even told my colleagues at lunch, "wait till you see – watch out for Jean, she will definitely want to put her oar in to destroy what I have to say".' Or you may think: 'I *knew* there was no use trying to bring in new ideas here, they never listen and of course they have no idea of the amount of work we have put into this.'

Notice how these thoughts are no longer connected to your project. They are all connected to your 'ego', your personal connection or identity with your project – the 'poor me' trying so hard …

As we saw above, passion creates energy and it helps you to think of new ideas and new ways to get to your goal. Emotion, however, creates stress, because the more we concentrate on our ability or inability to carry out a task, the more under pressure we become to succeed.

The problem is that being emotional directs us to focus on the wrong subject matter. Instead of focusing on the project itself, we focus on our ability to do the project. Instead of focusing on the issue, we focus on our ego. Instead of moving towards our goal, we move further away from it.

The following illustration shows how, even though our hearts may be pounding for what we want, to focus with emotion may be more dangerous than to focus with passion.

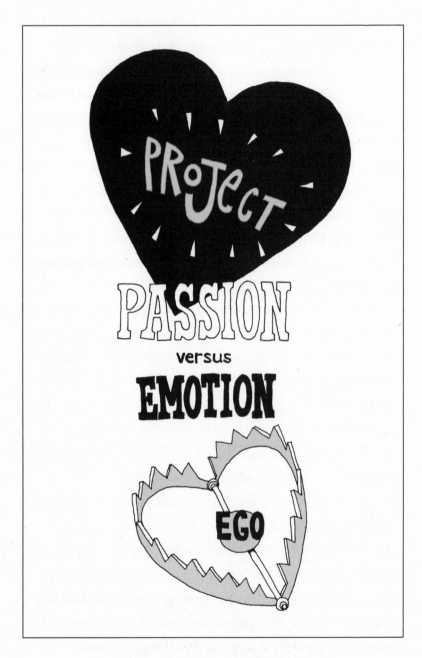

Figure 6: Passion versus Emotion

HOW DO WE FIND PASSION NOT EMOTION?

I'd like you to think back to the last time you ran a project. Do you remember if you were passionate about what you were doing – or were you emotional?

If you were passionate, you would have been able to hear criticism as a way of improving the project. When you encountered obstacles, you would have been able to think of numerous ideas to overcome these obstacles. Congratulations if you were able to think in this way! Focusing with passion gave you greater energy to reach your goal.

However, if you were emotional about your project, you may well have felt that you were very passionate about what you were doing, but the difference would have been where your thinking was focused. Was it directed towards the project or to yourself? Did you hear criticism as a means of improving what you were doing, or did you tend to hear criticism as a slight on yourself? If we are emotional, we will hear criticism as directed at ourselves and our ability to do our work. If we continue to focus on ourselves and our defence of our own egos in this way, then it is much more likely that we will become overwhelmed by our problems – and so the creative problem-solving process that we so need to succeed is not there and, instead of creating energy, we will create stress.

But don't worry, even if this was the case in the past,

even if you were more emotional than passionate, you can learn to become more aware of yourself and your motivations so as to successfully refocus to reach that goal you always wanted.

Here is a small test to start off the process – to see if you are passionate or emotional.

Think of a project you are working on at the moment or a goal you would like to reach. Now please answer these ten simple questions to see if you are passionate or emotional about what you want. For the best results it is important to try to answer them as honestly as you can.

1. Are you excited by your project? Yes/No
2. Do you feel challenged by it? Yes/No
3. Is the goal of the project clear to you? Yes/No
4. Does it fit with your values? Yes/No
5. Do you feel you have enough freedom to reach the project goal? Yes/No
6. Do you have enough support? Yes/No
7. Are you recognised for the work you do? Yes/No

How do you react to criticism?

8. Do you understand it as attached to the project? Yes/No
9. Do you understand it as attached to you? Yes/No
10. Do you work well with other members of the team? Yes/No

How did you get on? On balance, does your project make you feel energised or stressed?

If you answered yes to the above questions (except No. 9), you are definitely very passionate about your project and so will have completed the survey feeling very energised and in the mood to start thinking creatively about what you want. If, however, you answered no to most of the above questions, you may feel that you are more stressed about your situation and it might be necessary for you to see what you can do to overcome any of these issues that are stopping you from being at your best.

It will be very difficult for you to begin the first step of Clear Focus if your energy is being distracted to saving your ego over your project. Look at your motivations. What is most important to you? Are you motivated by fear? Do you feel in control or out of control? Remember that four-and-a-half-year-old who was afraid of the dark? There was nothing wrong with my environment. My fear and inability to focus became problematic because of my perception of my environment. Is your focus more on yourself and your fears, or have you taken the time to see, feel and touch every aspect of your environment outside yourself that might help you to solve your problems and reach your goal? Have you focused enough on what is outside you as well as inside you? Have you focused enough on the bigger picture around you?

CASE HISTORY: JOE

This is a story of a company director, Joe, whose fear of losing his business makes him blind to the bigger picture and the current opportunities in his environment. His is an example of wrong focus that might lose him the very thing he needs to sustain.

Joe's goal: to get money in so as to keep the company afloat. He is a director of a builders' provider with a number of stores countrywide. The company is going through tough economic times and it has been difficult over the past few years to generate sales and to get previous customers to pay their bills. In fact it has been a constant struggle to chase payments over a long time now. Joe's focus is to save the business. But because he is emotional (driven by fear of his own failure and lack of abilities) and not passionate (driven by his desire to save the business wherever he can spot opportunities) he believes that the way to save the company is to do everything in his power to retrieve overdue payments.

Using his own valuable time as a leader of his organisation, Joe drives long distances alone around the country, attempting to collect payments from individual customers in their own homes and businesses. This focus is limited and blinds Joe from seeing the bigger picture of an improving DIY economy. What he does not notice, even though his staff continuously tell him so, is the substantial pick-up in current customer footfall at each branch now that young people are beginning to buy older houses and need to do them up.

His wrong focus, driven by fear of failure, fails to let him appreciate a new and vibrant market. A Clear Focus in the right place would allow him to visit all his DIY branches, look at the customers three rows deep in the shops around the country buying again, and to reorganise or increase staff numbers to deal with the new influx and so make greater, much needed, current profits. He would focus on the bigger picture of finding money using all opportunities and realise that it would be better to find it with the new customers who are paying, instead of wasting time with the old customers who might pay.

A classic case of Focus driven by emotion and not Passion, I'm afraid. Remember: to have Clear Focus we need to be able to see the bigger picture.

CASE HISTORY: MR MANOJ SANJEEWA

Here is a contrary example of Focus driven by Passion and not emotion, told to me by a Sri Lankan friend. Can you spot the difference between this and Joe's case?

Thirty-year-old Mr Manoj Sanjeewa was the proud owner of Sanjeewa Video, a record shop in Ahangama, about fifteen kilometres south of Galle in Sri Lanka. The small, well-stocked shop sold DVDs and cassettes, and provided a healthy income for Mr Sanjeewa's family.

Although he is now living a comfortable life with a new house and business, nine years ago things did not appear so bright for Mr Sanjeewa. Like so many people living in coastal Sri Lanka, he lost everything on 26 December 2004. His possessions were swept away by the tsunami: his house was destroyed and his business was ruined.

Mr Sanjeewa was left with the gruelling task of having to rebuild a life for his family of four. 'Initially, we stayed with friends for two months and then moved into a Sewalanka Foundation-constructed temporary shelter near Galle,' said Mr Sanjeewa. 'The shelter was only made of timber, but it was like a palace to me. It was mine. After moving into the temporary house with my family, I was eager to start earning money and to rebuild my life. I wanted to repay my friends the money that they had lent me.'

Sewalanka Foundation (a Sri Lankan development organisation that enhances the capacity of disadvantaged rural communities) provided Mr Sanjeewa with a Rs25,000 grant which allowed him to reconstruct his destroyed shop and to restock the shelves.

Since re-opening Sanjeewa Video, Mr Sanjeewa has not looked back:

> Running the record shop keeps me extremely busy, but I am pleased that business is thriving – and I've even expanded the operation to include video production.

The idea of making movies has always interested me, so I seized the opportunity and started producing DVDs about local Sri Lankan dance. I never would have guessed that the venture would be so successful and that my DVDs would be sold in shops throughout the entire country. The tsunami taught me that life is fragile and anything is possible and as a result I decided to pursue my much greater long-term interest of not only selling videos and DVDs, but of making them too. I am so happy where I am now.

Mr Sanjeewa could have remained very emotional about his plight (and who could have blamed him?), but instead he changed his focus to one of chasing his dreams. He was passionate about succeeding, both for himself and his family, and seized on the opportunity that the crisis gave him to achieve his ideal of not only selling DVDs but also making films and videos himself. Notice also that, by focusing on his goal and achieving it with Clear Focus and direction, he also achieved a much greater feeling of happiness and well-being.

Passion also creates possibilities in the workplace for us all. Passion is not just personal. Passion can be the lifeblood of successful teamwork and is the competitive weapon used by the most successful organisations in the world. I believe a successful organisation has a duty to keep people passionate at work, as passion leads to the innovation all great organisations crave.

Most people start off in their jobs with an ambition to thrive. We all know how passionate someone can be when joining an organisation and then how, sometimes only a few months later, we see that same person descending into emotional wreckage. This has happened not because of the individual's lack of engagement, but more because of the organisation's lack of recognition of their efforts. It is not just up to the individual to remain passionate about their work. Organisations need to keep people passionate about working towards strong future possibilities, possibilities that they can feel excited and motivated to reach.

Teresa Amabile, Edsel Bryant Ford Professor of Business Administration and Director of Research at the Harvard Business School, cites six levers she believes every organisation needs in order to allow people to remain passionate about their work and focused in such a way that they can achieve great things.[6] She describes creativity as the 'inner passion' to solve a problem and she sees this ability as a 'huge competitive weapon'. She says that, as far as possible, all organisations should strive to achieve the following six levers to attain passionate, motivated staff:

---

6 T. Amabile, 'How to Kill Creativity', *Harvard Business Review*, September 1998, pp. 77–87.

1. **Challenge**: staff members should be given a job or project that challenges their strengths.

2. **Freedom**: they need to have the freedom in their work processes to reach goals.

3. **Resources**: they need to be given the time and resources necessary to reach goals.

4. **Work Group Features**: all members of a team need to share the same excitement about the team goals, each respecting the knowledge of others.

5. **Supervisory Encouragement**: each team member needs to be publicly recognised for a job well done, and if criticism is required it should be carried out as a constructive form of feedback.

6. **Organisational Support**: above all, it must be apparent that focused, creative problem-solving is embedded in the culture of the organisation, with approval from the very top.

If we strive for focused teamwork with focused team players, each respecting each other, then we will succeed.

The following story is an example of a Clear Focus that allowed everyone to achieve their goals:

A few years ago, at the Special Olympics, nine contestants, all physically or mentally disabled, assembled at the starting line for the 100-yard dash. At the gun, they all started out, not exactly in a dash, but with a relish to run the race to the finish and win. All, that is, except one little boy who stumbled on the asphalt, tumbled over a couple of times and began to cry. The other eight heard the boy cry. They slowed down and looked back. Then they all turned around and went back. Every one of them.

One girl with Down's syndrome bent down and kissed him and said: 'This will make it better.' Then all nine linked arms and walked together to the finish line.

Everyone in the stadium stood up and the cheering went on for several minutes. People who were there are still telling the story. Why?

Because deep down we know this one thing. What matters in this life is more than winning for ourselves. What matters in this life is helping others to win, even if it means slowing down and changing our course.[7]

What an inspiring story of Focus and achievement! This story highlights how the Passion of and within the group was able to carry the emotional need of a member of that group, and helps to show how the synchronisation of group focus can create enormous power for the benefit of all.

At an individual level, you too can learn to focus in a way that overcomes your own personal hurdles,

---

7 This story can be found on numerous websites, and is generally attributed to Diane Berke.

as is demonstrated in the following story of a real-life business experience.

One of my colleagues described how, when she was setting out in her business over ten years ago, she spent a lot of time on the phone trying to convince people to buy her product. Usually with a new product she was able to translate only a minority of these calls into meetings. But once she got the consultation with a prospective client, she was able to persuade them to buy. This is what it is like for most people starting off in business. My friend was able to do this and concentrated her efforts on making each meeting turn into a profitable sale.

She had to go through many rejected calls to make one productive meeting. She understood this very clearly. However, she was astonished one day when an acquaintance said to her with the utmost sympathy, 'I just don't know how you can take the rejection.'

My friend was amazed. 'What rejection?' she replied. 'No one is rejecting me, they don't even know who I am, so how can they be rejecting me? They are saying no to my product. So what I do is listen, find out why my product doesn't suit them, and then work on redesigning what I have to offer in order to meet their needs. Their rejection of my product is actually a way of helping me to become more successful, as I can learn so much and become a lot more creative in what I do.'

That is Passion and not emotion. By not taking rejection personally, we are able to connect the rejection we experience to our project and not our ego.

If you find you are concentrating on yourself in any situation, remember to separate your ego from the issue and to refocus on the goal you are trying to achieve and how you are going to get there. Don't think: 'Will I be able to ...?' Think: 'How do I do ...?'

DETERMINE YOUR FOCUS

Remember the clock to help you see the bigger picture and choose a focus that you know is the very best for you:

- Make sure feelings and desires work for you, not against you.
- Have passion for your project as it creates energy: when you are passionate, your feelings are attached to your project – you create energy and overcome problems to reach your goal.

- Being emotional about your project creates stress: when you are emotional your feelings are attached to your ego and so create stress – you may become overwhelmed by problems and so not reach your goal.

- Make sure you are always passionate, never emotional.

Using your Passions to control your Emotions

I would like to offer a final story of how Directed Passion and Clear Focus on achieving a goal control emotions.

A man observed a woman in the supermarket with a three-year-old girl in her trolley basket. As they passed the confectionary aisle, the little girl asked for biscuits and her mother told her no. The little girl immediately began to whine and fuss and the mother said quietly, 'Now Kate, we just have half of the aisles left to go through. Don't be upset. It won't be long.'

Soon they came to the chocolates section and the little girl began to shout for chocolate bars, and when told she couldn't have any, began to cry. The mother said, 'There, there, Kate, don't cry – only two more aisles to go and then we'll be finished our shopping.'

When they got to the checkout till, the little girl immediately began to clamour for chewing gum and burst into a terrible tantrum upon discovering there'd be no gum purchased. The mother patiently said, 'Kate, we'll be through this checkout till in five minutes and then you can go home and have a nice nap.'

The man followed them to the car park outside and stopped the woman to compliment her. 'I couldn't help noticing how patient you were with little Kate,' he began. Whereupon the mother said, 'I'm Kate. My little girl's name is Millie.'

I hope you enjoyed Kate's story, as a dose of humour is often the best medicine when trying to remain focused.

YOUR FIRST STOP: THE 'PASSION' PLATFORM

It is now time to take a rest, to put down your book and step onto your first resting platform on your stairway to successful Focus. As you take your rest, you can reward yourself for committing to understanding this first skill of attaining Clear Thinking and Focus. Now you can take time out to reflect on what you have read up to this point and how it can help you in your life. And it is here where you may want to create a plan to practise your skill of being passionate, never emotional.

You may find that you have read all you need to know at this point in the book, and that is okay. Knowing how to be passionate and not emotional may be all you need for now and, therefore, you can be satisfied that you have what you want to achieve your goals. Sometimes we need only one simple step to get where we want to go.

If you are leaving for now, I look forward to seeing you again soon if you decide to up-skill and move on to the next, more difficult steps of Clear Thinking and Focus.

Top Tip to be Passionate:

Concentrate on where you are strong
– not where you are wrong

6

Your Second Learning Curve: Productivity

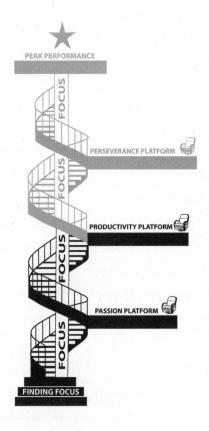

We will start these next steps with the assumption that your Focus is aligned to achieving your goal: you are passionate about achieving what you want and your critical and reflective thinking is focused on what you need to do. With this mindset you are ready to build on your next main strength to achieve your goal: your Productivity.

To begin these steps of the next learning curve, I would like you to reflect on the type of person you feel you are when faced with obstacles. To help you with this reflection, imagine you are sitting back and relaxing on your ongoing steps on your spiral staircase reading this lovely story.

Are you sitting comfortably? Then we'll begin:

A young woman went to her mother and told her about her life and how things were so hard for her. She did not know how she was going to make it and wanted to give up. She was tired of fighting and struggling. It seemed that as one problem was solved, a new one arose.

Her mother took her to the kitchen. She filled three pots with water and placed each on a high fire. Soon the pots came to a boil. In the first she placed carrots, in the second she placed eggs and in the last she placed ground coffee beans.

She let them sit and boil, without saying a word. In about twenty minutes, she turned off the burners. She fished the carrots out and placed them in a bowl. She pulled the eggs out and placed them in a bowl. Then she ladled the coffee out and placed it in a bowl. Turning to her daughter, she asked, 'Tell me, what do you see?'

'Carrots, eggs and coffee,' the young woman replied. The mother brought her closer and asked her to feel the carrots. She did and noted that they were soft. She then asked her to take an egg and break it. Having pulled off the shell, she observed the hard-boiled egg. Finally, she asked her to sip the coffee. The daughter smiled as she tasted its rich aroma.

The daughter then asked, 'What does it mean, mother?'

Her mother explained that each of these objects had faced the same adversity – boiling water – but each reacted differently. The carrot went in strong, hard and unrelenting. However, having been subjected to the boiling water, it softened and became weak.

The egg had been fragile. Its thin outer shell had protected its liquid interior. But, having sat through the boiling water, its inside became hardened!

The ground coffee beans were unique, however. After they were in the boiling water, they had changed the water.

'Which are you?' the mother asked her daughter. 'When adversity knocks on your door, how do you respond? Are you a carrot, an egg or a coffee bean?'

Think of this: Which am I? Am I the carrot that seems strong but, with pain and adversity, do I wilt and become soft and lose my strength? Am I the egg that starts with a malleable heart, but changes with the heat? Did I have a fluid spirit but, after a death, a breakup or a financial hardship, does my shell look the same, but on the inside am I bitter and tough with a stiff spirit and a hardened heart? Or am I like the coffee bean? The bean actually changes the hot water, the very circumstance that brings the pain. When the water gets hot, it releases the fragrance and flavour.

If you are like the bean, when things are at their worst you get better and change the situation around you. When the hours are the darkest and trials are the greatest, do you elevate to another level? How do you handle adversity? Are you a carrot, an egg or a coffee bean?

(Ancient Fable – author unknown)

How did you get on? Do you recognise yourself? Perhaps you find that you may be all of these entities in various situations, at different times – but do you notice a tendency for one type of reaction?

Knowing which type you are is an important piece of self-awareness to have in your toolkit as you tackle your ambitions.

To be at your most productive when you are focused on reaching your goals, it is important to know how well you can handle adversity. Negative thoughts will be automatic so they are not to be discarded. They are necessary even as a simple survival mechanism. For when we are in danger we need to feel fear to get a full understanding of the threat the situation poses for us. But it is how we handle these negative emotions and how we make them work for us that will decide our ability to focus or to simply give up.

USE NEGATIVE THINKING TO PRODUCE POSITIVE ACTION

Once we know that we are passionate about what we want to achieve, this focus helps us to achieve the more difficult second step in Clear Thinking – using our negative thinking in an intelligent way to transform it into positive action. Because, yes, negative thinking does not always have to end up as negative feelings or negativity. There is a way to focus with negative thinking and to understand it as a beacon of light and information that is trying to show us our way. If we learn to focus in a certain way, our negative thinking can help us to overcome problems and not be overwhelmed by them. Far from negative thinking being bad for us, I believe it can be very good for us, if we can learn to use it in the right way.

Here is a lovely story to illustrate my point:

In ancient times, a king had a boulder placed on a roadway. Then he hid himself and watched to see if anyone would remove the huge rock. Some of the king's wealthiest merchants and courtiers came by and simply walked around it. Many loudly blamed the king for not keeping the roads clear, but none did anything about getting the stone out of the way.

Then a peasant came along carrying a load of vegetables. Upon approaching the boulder, the peasant laid down his burden and tried to move the stone to the side of the road. After much pushing and straining, he finally succeeded. After the peasant picked up his load of vegetables, he noticed a purse lying in the road where the boulder had been. The purse contained many gold coins and a note from the king indicating that the gold was for the person who removed the boulder from the roadway.

(Ancient Fable, 'The Obstacles in our Path', author unknown)

The peasant learned what many people never understand and what I want to underline very strongly! Every obstacle presents an opportunity to improve our condition.

It is strange how we run away from negative thinking, unable to see its value. For example, I often ask people at my training workshops: 'How does negative thinking affect you?' and 'How do you feel when people are negative at work or when they come out with negative comments?' Most of the time (at least 99 per cent of cases), they say it makes them feel very bad. Their thinking shuts down and they are not able to respond in a calm way to the negative thoughts. They feel crushed, they say, by people who are negative and it is hard to fight back or get their positive ideas or views accommodated or communicated. This perception seems to exist throughout society.

I feel that negative thinking has been hijacked by

modern psychology theorists and made to become the producer of negative emotions. It seems to be common today to focus on negative thinking as an illustration of an erroneous type of thinking that has affected us at both a conscious and an unconscious level. Under this thinking we are doomed from childhood events or instances to be forevermore in its fierce, negative grip. Because our negative thoughts often spring from our unconscious or dormant subconscious, we cannot directly and rationally work through them unless we are made consciously aware of them as thoughts to be 'dealt with' and 'overcome' with the assistance of a psychological theory. I am being extreme here to make my point, but my mantra is simply that we do not have to consider negative thoughts as something we need to change in order to be happy.

My belief is that we should be able to focus on negative thinking or negative thoughts in a much more intelligent and helpful way. I have confidence that, if we do this, we can use them as the vital pieces of information that we need to be successful and will recognise them as very valuable ideas helping us to progress well throughout life. I believe it is wrong to regard negative thinking as erroneous thinking and something to overcome. It is my experience that negative thinking can give us the vital information we need to achieve exactly what we want.

Let me tell you a personal story to illustrate my

idea. It is about a negative incident that happened to me – one where I first discovered, very consciously and overtly, that without negative thinking I could not get anywhere.

I call this 'my bag story'. This negative situation may have happened to you too – in fact I think many people will identify with this story.

My story goes back to a few years ago. It happened on a lovely July evening. I had just flown from Dublin to Gatwick Airport, arriving at about 7 p.m. I was very excited that evening as the purpose of my trip was to give a talk at a conference in the south of England. This was a very prestigious event and I was thrilled that I had been asked to give a one-hour presentation on 'Clear & Critical Thinking' at 11 a.m. the following day. It was quite a hectic trip since, after my talk, I was to fly back to Dublin at 2 p.m.

This conference was a very posh affair and so I had packed my most beautiful power suit (bought specially to impress) with all my marketing papers for distribution. Indeed the event was so upmarket that there was a chauffeur waiting to collect me at the airport to drive me to my venue.

Imagine my horror as I stood by the luggage conveyor belt waiting for my bag to appear. Five minutes went by. Okay, no rush yet. Ten minutes and other people were retrieving their bags and disappearing out of the airport oblivious to my dilemma. Fifteen minutes and

I was beginning to panic, as I still did not see my bag appear. What was I going to do? I had to have my bag!

After twenty minutes I decided to do something. If I couldn't get my bag then I needed somebody who could. I went in search of the appropriate customer services person, who was very sympathetic, making all the right noises about how awful this must be for me not to have my bag, etc., etc. I can't stress enough to you that in Clear-Thinking terms, sympathy is the archenemy of action because it usually means 'no'. When people are sympathetic to you it is because you cannot get what you want, so the more sympathy they heap on you the more likely it is that you will never have what you are looking for. So I told this lady, in the nicest possible way, that she had to stop the sympathy, as I really, really needed the bag.

When sympathy didn't work she went one grade higher to 'realism' in an attempt to convince me that I could not get my bag: 'I am so sorry, Madam, but we have to be realistic. I'm afraid we cannot get your bag this evening, it is impossible.'

I was relegated to the statistics of those with lost bags in various airports around the world. Because negative thinking and reasoning are so powerful they can make us believe that what we want is indeed impossible.

On her suggestion I was about to head off to the airport shops to see if I could buy some other wearable conference-type clothes and to email home for my marketing material to be sent to me. Then it suddenly dawned on me that the negative reasoning she was using to prove it was impossible to get my bag contained the very information I needed to retrieve it that night.

I asked her to repeat the reasons that made her believe we could not get the bag. She said, 'First, the offices in Dublin are now closed. Second, we have no carrier coming over this evening as our next available plane from Dublin to London is tomorrow morning. And finally, we have a "no same day" policy – meaning it is impossible to retrieve a lost bag on the same day, as our policy is not to guarantee a return within the first twenty-four hours.' All of this led her very firmly to the conclusion: 'It is therefore impossible to have your bag tonight.'

I have portrayed this in Figure 7 for clarity and to show how negative reasons may look like they must lead to a negative conclusion.

**May I get my bag tonight? –
No, because**

- **Offices in Dublin are closed**
- **No carrier**
- **No same day policy**

= NO BAG TONIGHT

Figure 7: The Lost Luggage Problem

Most people would have given up at this stage and, to be honest, I was about to. Then I realised that perhaps what was going on here was not negative but positive, as her negative reasoning was the *key* to achieving what I wanted.

I quickly asked the airline official if she had a list of the offices in Dublin so that I or we could phone them on the off-chance that one might be open. She gave me the list – there were only three – and I offered to make the calls with her beside me. This would not cost her anything and we could become a team in solving the issue. We began to telephone and, astonishingly, somebody answered the phone.

It is important to note how relevant and informative this first negative barrier was in this story and why the airline lady used this reason – 'the office in Dublin is closed': it was based on her knowledge around what is normally required to retrieve an airline bag. She knew she couldn't get the bag if the office was closed because she knew she needed an open office to source the bag, retag the bag and put it back in the system. I had no idea of this. Therefore the negative thinker in negative situations may be the very one who has all the knowledge and the answers.

We had overcome our first hurdle – we had the open office in Dublin. My airport accomplice sourced the bag, got it retagged and put back in the system. It was then put on a different, sister company carrier, to London.

Now, thanks to negative thinking we had been able to carry out two actions that had my bag hurtling across the Irish Sea from Dublin to London at 500 m.p.h.

Once we knew the bag was safely on its way to Gatwick Airport, to arrive within the hour, the airline official completely ignored the 'policy' arrangement, as it now made no sense to keep the bag until the next day. I received my bag that night at 10 p.m.

Thanks to our ability to use negative thinking as much-needed information to solve the problem, and thanks to our ability to see the intelligence behind negative thinking, I was able to do something that was thought to be impossible.

One of the most amazing facets of negative thinking is how focused it makes us. Focus is the backbone of negative thinking – or is negative thinking the backbone of Focus? Either way, they are related. I was utterly focused in that airport, as was my helper. Instead, however, of negative thinking focusing us in a way that paralysed us, it focused us in a way that motivated us into action.

I am reminded of the phrase 'Never waste a good crisis', as the beauty of my bag story not only brought me relief at the moment of retrieving my lost possession, but also produced a moment of satisfaction for the airline official, who told me of her pride in being able to solve the kind of problem that all too frequently descended into horrible emotional entanglements with customers.

To make the impossible possible there is a simple phrase to help you focus your best thinking on reaching your goals. It is 'No, because = Yes, if' and, as we can see in the visual below, it was this way of thinking that brought about the solution to my bag dilemma.

To Get Things Done
No, because = Yes, if

- **Offices in Dublin are open**

- **We get a different carrier**

- **We get rid of policy**

= Bag at 10 p.m.

Figure 8: Solving the Lost Luggage Problem

When you have a negative thought it is important to ask yourself: 'What is this really telling me?'; 'What kind of knowledge or intelligent information can I find in this thought to help me?'; 'Can I turn a "no because ..." into a "yes, if ..."?' Or, 'Can I see a list of "why nots" to do something as an action plan of how to achieve it?'

To help you work through these questions and find positive and sustainable actions, let us return to the

DNA model thinking technique we saw work so well in the museum example above (page 33).

As you practise it here, it will show you step-by-step how to utilise negative thinking to your advantage. This DNA thinking technique is a vital part of your Focus 'Toolkit', since being able to use negative thinking in an intelligent way is often the most difficult part of remaining focused, given our tendency to anticipate obstacles when overcoming problems. We often lapse into emotional reasoning, perhaps fuelled by fear, uncertainty or doubt – the nagging thought that maybe we just might not be able to make it. It is here that the passion we once had for achieving our goals can disappear amongst the many overwhelming difficulties we encounter when trying to reach them.

Because of this danger, many people believe more in the power of positive thinking. In problem-solving or goal-setting we tend to love positive thinking, since exploring our options in a creative way can often make us incredibly positive and even giddy about achieving our aims. It is only when we reach the stage of separating the good ideas from the more difficult ones at the implementation stage that we descend into believing all is impossible. That is because the most attractive ideas are often the most difficult to implement.

Obstacles are often viewed as impossible and then seen as enormous blocks to transforming creative ideas into action – just think of the 'yes, but ...' factor. How many of us have cringed when we have brought good ideas to a meeting only to be told, 'oh, yes, that's a great idea, but we just don't have the budget at the moment', or 'oh, yes that's a great idea, but we don't have the resources', etc., etc. Most of us have an emotional reaction to these statements and retreat back into our shells so that nothing gets done.

However, as we have seen in my airport example, the best way to use negative thinking is to see it as a signpost, and not a block, to obtaining real action. With this information we can use our imagination and creativity to put in place a means of dismantling these obstacles and so achieve our goal.

To gain the most from Clear Focus and creative ideas, for example, the best way to order your thoughts is to model them under the DNA print model. This means that we devise a simple template that shows what we want, why we are not getting it and what we are going to do about that.

(D) Dream: your purpose.

(N) Negatives: the reasons you believe you can't achieve it.

(A) Actions: how you are going to overcome them.

Like your own DNA print is your unique identity mark, so too is the DNA print of your negative thoughts. This

DNA model helps you to use your negative thoughts because they are exclusive to you – they are your unique signposts to place you on your unique journey.

When working with this DNA thinking model it is very important that you remember three things to make it successful:

1. You must have a clear goal.

2. Allow your negative thoughts to flow out of your mind in any random order. As you feel them, write them down.

3. Before you begin to work on overcoming your negative thoughts, it is extremely important to rank them, from the easiest negative to deal with first, down to the most difficult. Your obstacles are then considered and ranked in descending order of how easy they are to overcome.

For example, if you wish to give a confident presentation on persuading others to implement an idea, you might say to yourself: 'I cannot do so for four reasons: (1) not enough time, (2) lack of information, (3) lack of confidence in my ability to present and (4) lack of coaching/training on effective presentations'. I would ask you to rank your 'obstacles' in descending order of easiest to tackle. Your list would then look something like:

1. I don't have enough information.
2. I don't have the time.
3. I have no access to a coach/training programme.
4. I worry about my ability.

The order is designed to produce momentum in the thought process, because as easier obstacles are cleared we become much more motivated in thinking creatively and so eventually produce many ideas to get rid of the very difficult ones. In many cases the most difficult obstacles fall away once we have thought of creative ideas to overcome the easy ones. In the above example, your worry about your ability (your most difficult obstacle) will be solved by successfully overcoming the previous obstacles. As you find answers to these easier obstacles, you will no longer worry about your ability. Thinking in this way has a critical impact on delivering your ideas into action.

DEVELOPMENT ACTIVITY

Think of a goal you would really like to reach. Now write down all the reasons why you are not achieving it. Be very specific and please be honest enough to write down all the reasons that are stopping you. (For example, some people who don't go to the gym will write down reasons that stop them, such as: 'It's too cold, I'm too tired, I don't have the right gear.' They find solutions for all these obstacles, but they still don't go to the gym. That is because they have not recorded or worked on the *real* reason why they don't go to the gym – i.e. *they don't want to!*) To change negative thinking into positive action, you must have the courage to record and work on the real reasons that are stopping action in order to tackle the real obstacles to your success.

On the left-hand side below, list the negative thoughts that are stopping you from achieving what you want. Make sure when you list them that you rank them, noting the easiest negative thought to overcome as No. 1, followed by the next easiest as No. 2, and so on. (It might be best to write them randomly first of all on a spare piece of paper.)

Your list of negatives (ranked)   **Your actions to overcome them**

1. _____   1. _____

2. _____   2. _____

3. _____   3. _____

4. _____   4. _____

5. _____   5. _____

When you feel you have listed enough – and you may have more than five – begin noting down your ideas, in the column on the right-hand side, on how to overcome each negative thought with a positive action.

When you have finished, stand back and notice

all the positive ideas you have come up with. Give yourself a pat on the back and enjoy the good feeling you are now experiencing. That good feeling comes with the ability to create productive ideas to move you forward.

When you have found the positive actions to overcome these negatives, write down the first action you will take to start you on your journey, with a time deadline, and enlisting the help of others if you need to.

My first action: _____

When: _____

With whom: _____

As you reflect on your positive use of negative thinking, I thought you might enjoy reading this DNA example story created by a group of unemployed young people in Dublin. These are the notes of the 'Dublin Job Club', an organisation that helps the young unemployed find work, and which was set up by Aaron Downes, an executive training consultant, in 2009, at the beginning of the recession. I ran a session with a group of these very enthusiastic youngsters, using the DNA thinking technique to find viable actions they could implement to reach their goal of finding gainful employment.

This is how our session worked. First of all we set out the dream, then we listed the reasons why they could not achieve their dream goal. Finally, we used creativity to overcome these barriers to achieve success.

(D) DREAM: to find work with good pay
(N) NEGATIVES: reasons why they could not achieve the dream:

1. Skills: under-skilled or over-skilled
2. Fear of rejection – disillusion
3. Efforts may not be fruitful
4. Limited thinking
5. Falling salaries in the market
6. Jobs not openly advertised
7. Financial pressure to take the wrong job
8. No jobs

(A) ACTIONS: by working on these negative thoughts, one by one, the group produced positive actions they could pursue to achieve their goal of finding work with good pay, as follows:

Negative 1. Skills: under-skilled or over-skilled

Under-skilled

- Up-skill for one to two years to be ready for a good job in the recovery.
- Make sure courses pursued are appropriate to the industry.

- Make ourselves more marketable by having extra qualifications.
- Gain work experience with courses (to get a foot in the door).

Over-skilled

- Widen category.
- Tailor CV to suit job.
- Use skills to create new potential work.

Negative 2. Fear of rejection – disillusion

- Keep up activities of searching for work.
- Put together a daily job plan (business development plan) to make our job seeking our own personal 'business'.
- Read widely.
- Ensure rejections make us more determined to get work.
- Count our blessings.
- Create a positive list.
- Create new questions.

Negative 3. Efforts may not be fruitful

- Change our attitude: questions, manner.
- Change how we do things – change the venues where we seek work, the type of work we seek, etc.
- Post on the Dublin Job Club (DJC) blog.

- Contribute to the DJC blog.
- Ask 'why' at interviews when not successful, and learn from the responses.

Negative 4. Limited thinking

- Talk to others about how they got jobs.
- Network.
- Set goals and test weekly where we are achieving on these goals.
- Brainstorm.
- Avoid negative influences.
- Create a new language to develop new thinking.

Negative 5. Falling salaries in the market

- Accept this reality.
- Acknowledge that costs are falling also.
- Work out a budget.
- Find new providers for our bill paying.
- Think long-term prospects.
- Look at government grants:
  o Enterprise Ireland
  o Enterprise boards.
- Negotiate remuneration according to excellent performance (be creative).

Negative 6. Jobs not openly advertised/not real

- Eliminate wrong searches that waste time.
- Target (only) the business we require.

- Join LinkedIn or other social media groups to widen our geographic job location possibilities.
- Create a real plan to target real jobs.

Negative 7. Financial pressure to take the wrong job

- Control financial outgoings.
- Change lifestyle – do simple stuff with no or low cost.
- Be creative with finances.
- Barter with other professions for needs.
- Use all facilities – source and resource.

Negative 8. No jobs

- Many in the group felt that if all the actions cited above were carried through, then the most difficult negative to overcome – no jobs – would not exist, as they will already have been successful at finding jobs given the above actions.

I am happy to report that with this focus and ability to analyse their negative thoughts and systematically produce solutions to tackle them, these young people found the answers to motivate themselves to achieve employment. Some set up their own small enterprises, while others job-shared and more found conventional jobs in the corporate sector.

Notice how they followed the rules of the DNA

technique to build on their motivation. They began by working on solving the easiest negatives first. Once they could find answers to these, their success gave them the awareness to know that they could perhaps also overcome the greater obstacles. More importantly, it gave them the motivation and energy to progress further. As their thinking progressed to tackling the more difficult negative thoughts, they could see that solving the earlier and easier negatives had a way of motivating their thinking skills to achieve greater and more complex solutions.

This pattern is very common in our everyday life. You have probably noticed that if you are able to solve a small problem, this effort alone gives you much greater confidence to tackle larger problems. A course participant at a recent workshop told me how this type of training is used in certain army personnel learning situations. His example was:

> In the army, we are not trained to escape if we fall behind enemy lines. This might sound strange, but to try to escape the enemy straightaway is too difficult. What we are trained to do is to attempt to achieve some quick wins – to achieve some success in overcoming smaller obstacles and so build up our motivation to escape. If we can overcome smaller obstacles, like receiving water or some other small concession, and succeed at that, we can gain momentum to build ourselves up for more difficult obstacles.

Through working on motivating your thinking in this challenging way you can reach the highest level of thinking ability. Instead of simply surviving from crisis to further crisis, with practice at overcoming challenges in this way you can reach a mode of thinking that is called 'Competency Mode', which is much more than a simple survival skill.

I first came across this distinction when I heard it presented by Michael Carroll, a lecturer on the AMEC programme (MSc in Executive Coaching) at the Ashridge Business School in England. Michael, in a personal communication, talked about two different modes of living and learning as the brain goes through change. One is called 'Survival Mode', the second is 'Competency Mode'. To be really focused and able to act to your advantage and to progress, you clearly need to be in Competency Mode. The difference between the two is stark. Survival mode, despite its title, is not good. If you are in survival mode you certainly will not be able to focus. In order to have Clear Focus and the power to act you must be in competency mode. The reason is the difference between the two.

In survival mode our actions are ones of:

❖ Fight
❖ Flight
❖ Fragment or
❖ Freeze.

These are actions that are simply reactions. They are non-thinking and so are not able to sustain our focus on achieving what we want. In survival mode we are not in control, as we are propelled from one environmental reaction to another.

To remain focused, with Clear Thinking towards achieving our goals, we need to be able to enter our competency mode. Competency mode is the ability to be in control of our living and learning so as to be able to achieve what we desire.

In competency mode our actions consist of:

❖ Reflection (managing emotions)

❖ Imagination

❖ Creativity

❖ Reasoning

❖ Problem-solving and solution-finding.

And it is this competency mode that I am asking you to step into now as you arrive at the last learning curve and reach towards your full potential. Here you will learn the ultimate in remaining focused as we work through the essentials of being able to think clearly 'in the moment', when you need it most of all to achieve your goals. At this level of Focus I will introduce you to other people's tricks of manipulation that may confuse your thinking. You will learn how to spot thinking errors that muddle thinking and so confuse you when making strong decisions to sustain your desires. However, before we arrive at that place, we have reached our second resting platform – our Productivity platform.

YOUR SECOND STOP:
THE 'PRODUCTIVITY' PLATFORM

This platform is where you can put down your reading and reflect on how to implement the learning and ideas you have just digested.

As you rest, you can reward yourself for committing to understanding, not only the first skill of using your passions to control your emotions, but for having added the second and more difficult skill of turning negative thinking into positive action.

Now you can take time out to reflect on what you have read up to this point and how it can help you in your life. And it is here where you may want to create a plan to practise your second skill of changing negative thinking into positive action.

You may find that you have read all you need to know at this point and that is okay. Knowing these first and second skills of Clear Thinking and Focus may be all you need for now and, therefore, you can be satisfied that you have what you want to achieve your goals.

If you are leaving for now, I look forward to seeing you again soon if you decide to up-skill and move on to the next and final learning curve.

We will start this next step with the assumption that your focus is aligned to achieving your goal, you are passionate about achieving what you want and you are a champion at critical and reflective thinking – being especially brilliant at turning negative thinking into positive action.

With this mindset you are ready to build on your next and final strength to achieve your goal: Perseverance.

Top Tip to be Productive:
It's okay to be wrong and it's good to use negative thinking

YOUR THIRD LEARNING CURVE: PERSEVERANCE

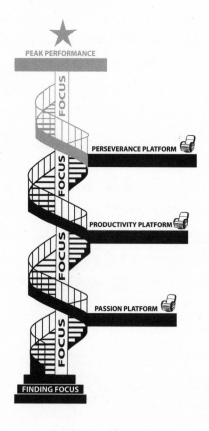

Congratulations for reaching the top level of your staircase. You are getting closer to your Peak Performance, where you will be able to use your 'spiral staircase wit'. It is not the one that you know how to use *after* the event, but the one that you will be able to use competently at the moment you most need it, during the event, discussion or meeting where you are determined to win that project or achieve the result you want.

By using your Passion and your Productivity you are well on your way to your full Clear-Thinking potential. Now is where you learn to overcome the most difficult thinking errors that hinder Clear Focus. It is here that you learn to depend on your Perseverance to be able to use 'cool logic in hot situations'. Using Perseverance at this stage means you are able to evaluate options so as to choose the one that is to your best advantage.

My aim in this chapter is to explain how you can recognise nine common thinking errors and overcome them with four required qualities of character: if you can deal with thinking errors 'in the moment', you will have the power of utter clarity and great personal influence. In other words you will be able to make a decision when you need to, based on sound and solid thinking.

Up to this point, with Clear Focus you have been able to fulfil the first two aspects of 'ACT'.

- *(A) Advance* towards your goal: by ensuring your passions control your emotions.
- *(C) Champion* your cause: by turning negative thinking into positive action.

Now it is time to:

- *(T) Take Control of your Actions:* this is where you

work on the most difficult and challenging aspect of Clear Thinking – that is your ability to think 'in the moment' and 'on the spot' to achieve your goals. Now is the time you will focus on your power to act.

NINE COMMON THINKING ERRORS THAT DISTRACT FROM CLEAR THINKING

The following are the nine most common thinking errors or tricks of manipulation that make us lose Focus. I have placed these nine errors under three simple headings – False Friends, Personal Attacks and Tired Thinking – that I hope will act as a good memory aid for you:

A. **False Friends** include:
   1) False Authority
   2) False Dilemma
   3) False Cause

B. **Personal Attacks** include:
   4) Abuse and Stereotyping
   5) FUDs (Fear, Uncertainty and Doubt)
   6) You're Wrong, so I'm Right

C. **Tired Thinking** includes:
   7) Jargon
   8) False Comparisons
   9) Repetition

FOUR QUALITIES YOU NEED TO OVERCOME THE NINE THINKING ERRORS

You may recognise some of these tricks or thinking errors by their simple titles. For readers familiar with my book *Quick Thinking On Your Feet*, you will notice that I am adding four qualities here that build on the information in my previous work. They are:

- ❖ Independence of Mind
- ❖ Courage
- ❖ Staying Power
- ❖ Big-Picture Thinking.

It is my role in this final 'learning curve' on your staircase to show you how you can achieve these qualities by working on the skills you need to overcome manipulation and resistance by others when you attempt to influence them.

The four qualities above are the antidotes to the muddled thinking and thinking errors you meet at this level in your ability to focus. Your powers of Focus will be tested, sometimes to the brink, but at this part of the staircase you will find the tools to make your way up to be at your best or peak performance.

This degree of Clear Thinking helps you to achieve a personal influence that is strong and calm and that creates a space of safety and shelter for others. As you can see in Figure 9 (overleaf), it is this ability to deal

Figure 9: The Umbrella of Personal Influence

with the muddled thinking behind 'ignorance', 'indifference', 'anger', 'blame' or 'confusion', that leads you to greater personal influence. The person who has this ability can act like a shield for others. The umbrella metaphor is interesting in that a person skilled in staving off confused or muddled thinking is able to stop these destructive forces 'raining down' on others, and in this way, is able to think at a higher level and bring others to think at that higher, clearer level also.

By thinking clearly you can cut through the constant clutter and background noise at meetings, and so keep yourself and all participants focused on what is most important to achieve.

So how do your four qualities work? Each has its own special job and each relates to what can be achieved by overcoming the thinking errors that lead to faulty decision-making and problem-solving. So you may be able to use 'Independence of Mind' to tackle the tricks of manipulation and false thinking, but you will also, without doubt, be building up your personal power, as you become more resilient to such obstacles.

- In overcoming and dealing with False Friends, you will achieve **Independence of Mind**.
- In overcoming and dealing with Personal Attacks, you will develop both **Courage and Staying Power**.
- In overcoming and dealing with Tired Thinking, you will illustrate **Big-Picture Thinking**.

So, with Clear Thinking you will have a twofold experience. On the one hand you will develop your analytical thinking skills, and on the other you will develop four very worthwhile personal qualities.

As shown in the story of myself as a six-year-old child and how excited I was to be challenged to put stones into a box (page 12), being focused can be a fun and enjoyable learning experience. It can challenge us in a way that we learn to develop ourselves and our qualities and abilities to a higher level – a level perhaps that we may not have even thought possible.

Remember, willpower isn't just a skill – it's a muscle. I hope you enjoy your journey as you strengthen it along the way.

How to achieve Clear Thinking in the face of the Nine Thinking Errors

This section aims to familiarise you with how the nine thinking errors manifest themselves and to give you options on how to remain calm and focused. Contrary to popular myth, being competent at Clear Thinking is not about being 'speedy' or 'up-to-the-minute' in knowing what to say and do. Quick thinking is more often displayed and illustrated by a very calm presence.

You will notice colleagues or friends who remain focused at meetings displaying great calm, interest in staying on the topic and reaching conclusions that are best for all. To be efficient at Clear Thinking means sometimes not saying very much. Success is being able to stay still when others are reacting or overreacting to input that makes no sense.

When you want to remain focused, the best thing to do is to take a deep breath to give yourself time to think and not react.

To assist your learning I have devised the following format. For each thinking error you will find:

- ❖ A description of how it occurs.

- ❖ A guided response: how you can 'respond with confidence'.

- ❖ An exercise: an example of real life stories and dilemmas containing the error for you to comment on. My answers will also be given, but I would like you to give your response first, before you look at mine.

- ❖ A personal worksheet: to record your own challenges and responses so as to flex your own Clear-Thinking muscles.

We will also be looking at some thinking errors in the form of two quizzes, so you can enjoy different modes and styles of learning.

Some of these problem situations are those sent to me by people in ordinary work situations in my capacity as agony aunt for a magazine titled *WMB* – 'Women mean

Business' (see www.womenmeanbusiness.com). They are genuine issues that I believe are very common, so I think you will identify very easily with them and that they can form good exercises for you to grasp the meaning of the errors of thinking and manipulation that cloud our Focus and Clear Thinking.

We don't have to agree on our answers. There are many right answers to these thinking errors and many different ways of overcoming them. I hope you can add your own ways of handling them to mine so as to build up your individual and personal learning toolkit.

A note of caution on how you deal with manipulation: in a general sense it is best not to react to these tricks by trying to hit them 'head on' so to speak. Clear Thinking is not about being 'right' and making sure everyone else knows that too! Clear Thinking is about knowing what to focus on and staying on that path. There is wisdom in Clear Thinking that allows us to see what is most important in every situation and how to remain focused in order to achieve it. Like a good chairperson at a meeting, our ability to succeed is based on knowing the end goal and making sure that we do not get diverted along the way. I will say it again – the best way to handle any distractions or diversions in thinking is to remain calm – always. If you try to show someone up for using these thinking errors, then you might find that you have a more difficult situation on your hands. For sometimes (not always) people are unaware that they are manipulating a situation by thinking incorrectly. Sometimes they are completely unaware and *they* may feel attacked if you try to point out what they are doing.

> By showing a man that he is wrong, and that what he says and thinks is incorrect … you embitter him more than if you use some rude or insulting expression.
>
> Arthur Schopenhauer, 'The Art of Always Being Right', in *Parerga and Paralipomena (1851)*

If you wish to influence others for the best it is very important to remember that for the strongest results, no matter how strong you are, you will need to treat others, and especially their egos, with the greatest of respect.

As you will see from Figure 10 (overleaf), even though, with your splendid thinking, you may feel as large as a ship navigating through simple patches of choppy or icy water, never forget the story of RMS *Titanic* and how an iceberg was able to destroy a craft that was thought to be invincible. Likewise, what you might think of as small shattered egos, in any challenging Change Management situation, can or might destroy you.

Treating others with kindness and respect is very important. When you encounter manipulation, when you are dealing with faulty thinking, you don't know

Figure 10: Sailing through the 'Icy Sea' of Egos

whether you are dealing with accident or intention, so it is best that you remember to be passionate and focused on your goal to achieve what you want, as it can be so easy to become side-tracked in defending your *own* ego.

The easiest way to remain focused when all around you are losing their focus is to recognise the power in yourself to remain calm and to never lose focus on the issue. The golden rule is to never be diverted by egos – especially your own.

HOW TO DEAL IN DETAIL WITH THINKING ERRORS

FALSE FRIENDS

1) False Authority – Antidote: Independence of Mind
How it Occurs
'False Authority' can come in two guises:

❖ Tradition

❖ The Power of the Group.

Thinking based on good traditions, practised by a majority of successful communities, is an essential way of how we function at our best as the human race. But it is also why, when we meet the weight of 'tradition' or 'the power of the group' as thinking errors, that we may be hoodwinked into thinking they are sound.

For example, tradition is how good practices are

handed down from one generation to another – practices that have worked well in the past and so *must* be passed on for survival. Examples abound around finding food, clothing and shelter. The power of the group is how modern Western democracies work (or are supposed to work!), where actions and people are voted in or out depending on the majority wish. The assumption is that if a majority believes in something it must be best for that majority. This may work if what we are voting for is genuinely good and, as with the examples given of tradition, it works if the action being passed on is genuinely worthwhile for our survival.

The thinking error, however, occurs in 'False Authority', when the first basic premise is faulty. That is, if those using this bias of tradition or the power of the group are attempting to force through an action which is not genuinely sound and they believe that by making it look like good tradition, or by making believe that 'everyone thinks it is good', these thoughts alone will make it worthwhile. In other words, there is no proof for the soundness of the idea – it is just dressed up to look good with juicy hearsay and spicy opinions!

You may come across this in the workplace as a 'we've always done it this way' type of argument. In a situation where people are afraid to change, this is usually the first line of defence and if they can muster up enough support, they may add on the power of the group syndrome to make it very much stronger. As in: 'You are the only one here who believes this practice needs to be changed – we have always done it this way for many years and everyone knows how good it is and that we would be mad to do anything differently, etc.'

Can you feel the strength of it even when reading it here? It is powerful, so what do we do?

Guided response: to respond with confidence

One way is to praise your colleague for making good past decisions based on the information they had at that time. Then find ways to stress the consistent values that connect their previous actions and products with your values now underlying the new actions, changes and products. In this way you are *complementing* their thinking and not contradicting it, which is always much easier to warm to. For example if you wish to introduce a new system and your colleagues don't want to change because their system is very fast or saves money, then you show that your system will be even faster, save more money, etc.

Secondly it is important to note that the strengths of these arguments are only based on opinions and not on facts. If this speaker were to continue by giving us the facts and figures around why the idea or work practice was a good one, then it would no longer be a thinking error.

The problem with opinions is that they can often

cloud facts and become psychologically more powerful than evidence-based facts and so distort our thinking. Below is an example of a reader who wrote to my agony aunt column with her problem. Try to identify what her thinking error is and give her some options to finding a solution.

Exercise

Dear Valerie,

I work for a well-known bank and I recently got my six-month work review. Going into the boardroom with my team leader and facing the big boss was not something that I'd prepared for! But all in all it went fine. My one issue is when I was asked to rate my level of work on the grades a, b, c and d, etc. I'm a good worker but I haven't been breaking my back to do the work and I've never stayed late so I decided to give myself the credible grade of c, which in our company is viewed well. It was only when I saw the shock on my boss' face that I figured my mistake! He told me that he had rated me a high b and he was quite concerned that I only rated myself a c. In the end he decided if that was all I thought I was worth then that is what he would put on my review. The annual salary review will be in January but I'm raging that I may have messed up my chances! Is there any advice you can give me?

Sylvia

Note your thoughts to Sylvia:

Dear Sylvia,

_____

_____

_____

_____

_____

_____

_____

_____

_____

_____

_____

_____

_____

_____

_____

_____

Yours sincerely,

The following is my answer to Sylvia.

Dear Sylvia,

I am so delighted that you learned this valuable lesson at a localised, interim work review. Performance reviews or annual salary reviews are never, and I mean *never*, based on opinion. A good review strives constantly to base its conclusions on factual information that can be tested and confirmed to be true.

Your boss may be helping you to see this by asking you your opinion at this interim level, and the good news is that you have the time to rectify your mistake before January.

First of all, remember it is very unwise to rate yourself on 'what I am worth'. Are you looking at too many ads? I wonder! Whenever anyone asks you to grade your own performance you must do that with regard to the shared objectives that are agreed at the beginning of the year, using work examples that correspond exactly to your job description and career framework.

Your salary is one of the most important assets of your life Sylvia, so let's see how we can ensure you get the best that is on offer. Here is some advice to help you in January at your annual review:

- Always keep in mind the huge importance of an annual salary review. It will decide how much money you can earn, and so is the ultimate goal of your career. Too many women rise up the ladder with far less pay than a man in a similar situation.
- Contact your HR department and ask for a meeting with a member of that department to outline with

you the exact work you must do to achieve 'excellent', 'well met' or other types of grades.

- Lastly, make sure you carry out these tasks and keep a diary of all the work you do between now and January next. Record work examples that show you have achieved the required grades.

If you carry out these three tasks, you will have factual proof at your annual salary review in January to show you are eligible for the salary you wish to achieve.

Good luck, Sylvia.

Notice that in this answer to Sylvia I have emphasised the difference between facts and opinions, which is essential for the disentangling of False Authority. Sylvia's thinking error is that her belief that she was not good at her job was based on her *traditional* opinions of what it means to be a good worker: 'staying late' or 'breaking her back'. As well, you will notice she gave herself a mark, 'a credible c', that she believed *the company would view well* (the power of the group), which is also another opinion. It is a simple but very powerful mantra always to separate fact from opinions when looking for true authority.

Sylvia's example is important to note so you can see that it is she who is using the thinking error of 'False Authority'. It is she who is both perpetrator and victim of this error and so cannot blame anyone else for her dilemma. It is important to remember that it is not only others who may manipulate us to come to false conclusions. We need to be vigilant as sometimes it is ourselves who may also be the cause of our own battles!

Personal Worksheet

Below is a worksheet for you to use to tell your own story of your experience with the thinking error of 'False Authority' in its two guises: 'tradition' or 'the power of the group', as it happened to you.

Challenge: Why did you feel the situation was a challenge? What was so challenging about it? Why was it *your* challenge?

_____

_____

_____

_____

_____

_____

_____

Choice: Why did you make the choice you did? How did it feel?

_____

_____

_____

_____

_____

_____

_____

_____

_____

Outcome: What was the outcome? How did it feel? What did it teach you?

_____

_____

_____

_____

_____

_____

_____

_____

Thinking Tip:
Understand and empathise with opinions, but always make your judgements based on facts

2) False Dilemma – Antidote: Independence of Mind
How it Occurs

Our second false-thinking friend comes in the guise of creating a False Dilemma for us. The well-known expression 'to be between a rock and a hard place'

Figure 11: Independence of Mind

is what the False Dilemma experience can make you feel like – caught, pressurised or paralysed so that you cannot think at all. When this happens your Clear Thinking leaves you and you revert back to 'survival mode' where you become reactive to circumstances as opposed to being reflective on your circumstances. You can go into the classic survival modes of being in flight mode, fight mode, fragmenting or freezing.

One description of this type of manipulation or thinking error is as follows. A False Dilemma arises when we allow ourselves to be convinced that we have to choose between two and only two mutually exclusive options, when that is untrue. Generally, when this strategy is used, one of the options is unacceptable and repulsive, while the other is the one the manipulator wants us to choose. Whoever succumbs to this trap has thus made a choice that is forced and, as such, of little value.

That is the one example of False Dilemma and perhaps it is the most obvious one. However, there are many variants of which you need to be aware.

- The irrational choice (as above).
- The rational choice (when it looks like you are being asked to make a choice between two equally desirable actions – however, you are only given two out of many, and these two have already been packaged for your approval).

- The 'you've already made a choice, so which one will it be' (as when you are asked in a shop, 'which size of dress would you like Madam' – this implies that you have already chosen to buy a dress).
- The either/or choice (as when you are made to believe that your choice is exclusive to one or other option only, when you could have both).
- The 'there is no choice' syndrome (as when we ask a child if they wish to go to bed at 6.00 or 6.30 – they are going to bed, whatever they choose …).

Again, some of these may be familiar to you and it might be interesting to stop here and notice which one in particular you find most difficult, or in fact which one you find you use more frequently than you would like to admit (especially if you have children!).

For example, I find the 'rational choice' in this type of thinking error the most difficult. Being a predominantly rational thinker, if I am given a choice between two equally desirable options, I tend to spend my thinking time trying to decide which one is best. It unfortunately does not dawn on me that there could be a third, fourth or even fifth option that I have not even considered.

Beware of the packaging of choice and always demand to be told whether there are more options. If you are given an already packaged choice, it is a sign that the person offering you the choice has already done the thinking for you and in this way is exerting a False Authority over you.

Guided response: to respond with confidence

The best way to overcome this manipulation of your thinking is to ask yourself if you are fully aware of all the options available to you. The best question to ask those who offer you limited either/or choices is one that will seek to find out what kind of extensive research they have carried out to reach these choices and this final conclusion of two.

You can also fall into this thinking error yourself when you are feeling emotionally drained by a certain situation. You may feel you have no options. You may feel trapped and think there is no way out. But again, it is your feelings that are tricking your thinking, because there is *always* another way that you have not thought of – our thinking is never exhaustive or exclusive. There are always new ideas and new ways we will not have thought of and our imagination is there for a purpose – to give us that ever-increasing power to search for more, better and wider choices. Please do use it.

Overleaf is an example of a reader who wrote to my agony aunt column with her problem. Sorcha is a small business owner. Try to analyse her thinking error and give her some options to finding a solution.

Exercise

Dear Valerie,

I've recently taken on someone for work experience to help out with some of the workload, and also to do a friend a favour. The new addition to the company is my friend's daughter. The problem is she's just not cutting it and I'd prefer to let her go sooner rather than later. She rarely answers the phone, takes numerous tea breaks and I find she's distracting my other employees with her chatter! How am I supposed to tell her it's not working out without letting down my friend who thinks there might be a job waiting for her daughter at the end of the six weeks?!

Sorcha

Your response to Sorcha:

Dear Sorcha,

_____

_____

_____

_____

_____

_____

_____

_____

_____

_____

_____

_____

_____

_____

_____

_____

_____

Yours sincerely,

My response:

Dear Sorcha,

Thank you for taking the time to write to me. I sympathise with your dilemma, but hope at the same time to show you that it is a false one. I think your dilemma is a particular female one in that, in my experience, more women than men mix friendships with business and can so easily find themselves in this type of situation, without realising why or how it has happened!

Your problem, Sorcha, is very aptly described in the first line of your letter. You say 'I've recently taken on someone for work experience to help out with some of the workload, and also to do a friend a favour.' Your action of taking on this young person had a dual purpose:

1.   To help out with some of the workload.

2.   To do a friend a favour.

For one action to have two purposes is a dangerous thing, as these are now competing with each other and causing you such conflict you cannot make a decision.

To overcome this dilemma you must decide which purpose here is the most important to you. To help you to answer, I believe it would be No. 1. You took on this young person to help out with some of the workload. Your other purpose to be nice and help out a friend is only secondary to that. Therefore your decision to keep on this young person, or let her go, must be based *only* on whether your expectations regarding your first and real purpose have been fulfilled. In other words, has this girl helped you out with the extra workload and do you think she will continue to do so in the future?

Reading the rest of your letter, the answer to that question does seem very unlikely to be 'yes'. You say she rarely answers the phone, takes numerous tea breaks and distracts your other employees. If your answer to the above question is no, then you must let her go.

With regard to your fear of letting down your friend, I believe this is also false reasoning. Because *you* are not letting your friend down. It is her daughter who is letting her down.

Think about it, Sorcha. You have done everything

possible to help out your friend, even to the point of giving her daughter this very valuable work experience. That is all you were asked to do. It was up to your friend's daughter to prove she could do the job and so achieve the permanent position you have on offer. Unfortunately, she has not been able to do that and so there is no job waiting for her at the end of the six weeks. She has been given the opportunity, that is all you promised to do, and you did it very generously. It is your friend's daughter who has not fulfilled her part of the bargain and, therefore, she cannot progress further.

I would have a very calm and friendly talk with your friend. Tell her you were delighted to help out her daughter with her work experience, but make it very clear that there is no job at the end of the six weeks. And I would make it very clear that your decision is based on her daughter's actions, not yours. You don't have to go into the details, but I would remain firm that the situation is how you describe it. If your friend's daughter cannot do the job, then it is best for her that she finds something else more suitable. In fact, you do not mention if your daughter's friend actually wants the job. Perhaps she may be delighted to move on herself!

Remember, Sorcha, your business cannot be a social service. You must keep a Clear Focus on running a profitable business that achieves its own strategic goals both for yourself and the good staff you have with you, and I am sure your friend will understand this, also.

Good luck,

Valerie

Did you notice the same errors as I did? If you are working in a group reading these exercises together, it might be interesting to have a discussion around the many complexities of this situation, which perhaps you and your friends may encounter when working with family and friends.

Personal Worksheet

Below is a worksheet for you to use to tell your own story of your experience with the thinking error of 'False Dilemma' as it happened to you.

Challenge: Why did you feel the situation was a challenge? What was so challenging about it? Why was it *your* challenge?

_____

_____

_____

_____

_____

_____

_____

_____

_____

_____

Choice: Why did you make the choice you did? How
did it feel?

_____

_____

_____

_____

_____

_____

_____

_____

Outcome: What was the outcome? How did it feel?
What did it teach you?

_____

_____

_____

_____

_____

_____

_____

_____

> **Thinking Tip:**
>
> *A choice is about choosing amongst many options –
> don't cheat yourself by creating limitations*

3) False Cause – Antidote: Independence of Mind
How it Occurs

You may have noticed that Sorcha's dilemma also had an aspect of False Cause in it, that is, the tendency to think that we are the cause of a problem, when in fact we are only caught up in the problem, playing a bit part in the sequence of events. Again a false friend in our thinking, and one that can cripple our thinking and bring it to a standstill.

We can become a victim to this type of false thinking when we feel particularly vulnerable or lacking in confidence. When we are in such a state we can easily assume that we are not in control of our thinking and so believe that we are the cause of anything and everything going wrong. In the workplace this can result in a blame culture becoming embedded. In an extreme example, it can lead to bullying if one person, department or sector is continually being blamed for low, or lack of, overall organisational performance. This thinking error is particularly powerful in bad times when everyone is searching for someone or something to blame for the lack of success. This form of manipulation destroys the ability to achieve Clear Focus to be able to solve the real causes of the problems and so find sustainable solutions to move on.

The fundamental flaw of False Cause is to believe that just because one event precedes another it means that the first action causes the second. To overcome this error of manipulation it is important to realise and remember that two actions can also come together in a simple sequence of events in time, without the first one causing the second, as in night following day, for example. We know that day does not cause night to happen, one just follows the other in a simple sequence of events.

However, in a work situation it is sometimes not so clear whether a preceding action caused a certain problem or not and so this thinking error can become very predominant in apportioning blame where there is none. For example, if you are a banker and you released a loan to a customer, and eighteen months later the loan goes bad and the customer defaults, you may be hauled into a meeting over your bad decision. But did the loan cause the default in payment? The second action could not have happened without the first, but it is faulty logic to conclude that the first action must have caused the second one. There could be many reasons why the customer defaulted, not connected to the decision to grant the loan.

At the time of securing the loan the customer would have passed all the required criteria to draw it down. S/he would have ticked all the right banking boxes and so the decision to grant the loan would have been a good one. At some later time a new variable entered the situation and was the cause of the loan now faltering. For example, the customer may not have reached sales targets or may have experienced credit control problems that could not have been foreseen at the time of the decision to loan (perhaps due to a bankruptcy of a connected creditor or other such examples).

If you find you are caught up in this type of thinking error, either instigated by yourself or others, it is important to stop for a moment to think in depth about how your actions are connected to your current problem. I say this error may be instigated by yourself or others, as we can often carry out this faulty thinking on ourselves when we believe we are the cause of some disaster because we are feeling guilty or believe we should have done more, etc. Guilt can be and should be a trigger to tell us we have done something wrong so that we can be alerted to change our behaviour (although sometimes I find that the greatest perpetrators of problem situations feel no guilt whatsoever!). However, because of lack of confidence some of us can think we are the cause of every disaster just because we happen to be in close proximity.

Guided response: to respond with confidence

To fix this error and refocus your thoughts on what is really happening in a given situation is very simple. All you need to do is ask the question: 'Where is the causal connection between this problem we are now facing and my preceding action or decision?' Remember, you can see the sequence of events – one action precedes another. The essential point, however, is to verify if one action caused the other.

If you are the victim of this manipulation by another, this question is the essential way to make sure you are not blamed for something you did not do. You should simply ask your accuser: 'That's interesting, how do you make the connection between this problem situation and my decision?' You must stop then and wait for their response. Do not try to justify your actions by saying, 'Okay, we have a problem here, but don't let us continue to analyse the whys and the wherefores, just let's concentrate our energy on fixing it' – to talk like this is to accept that you are responsible for the problem, when in fact no evidence was given that you are.

So, if you are accused, always throw out the question and wait for the accuser to justify their accusation. If they cannot, they are bluffing or using this thinking error, perhaps without realising it. It is up to you to point out that your actions are only part of a sequence of events and that your accuser must show you evidence of the causal connection. If, of course, your accuser can give you full evidence for you being the real cause of a problem, then they are not using manipulation here and you should say sorry instantly.

Here is an example of such manipulation in Mark's story. Read what he has to say and then as your exercise on this thinking error, I would like you to write what you could say to Mark to help him understand this flaw and what he could do in a similar situation in the future.

Mark is a maths teacher in a college catering for fifteen- to seventeen-year-olds. At a certain time there was industrial unrest in the school and the teachers decided to go out on short one- and two-day lightning strikes during the months of February and March: a total of four days was taken. The following September there was a serious drop in the number of new students. A meeting was called, during which one chap stood up and made a very impassioned speech about how he knew they should never have gone out on strike. 'Look at the damage the strike has caused,' he said. Because they were all feeling so guilty about having gone out on strike, everyone in the room was transfixed. No one thought to ask: 'Is there a valid connection between the strike and the drop in numbers?' Mark told me afterwards that when they did look into the matter in more detail, they found there were several other reasons, factors and variables for the drop in student intake.

What is interesting in this story, and what made Mark very aware of this trick for the future, was that he saw at first-hand how an intelligent group of people, because of guilt, became powerless to think clearly when confronted by this particular form of manipulation. It is very powerful and hits the emotions very hard indeed.

Exercise

What would you say to Mark to help him respond correctly 'in the moment'?

Dear Mark,

_____

_____

_____

_____

_____

_____

_____

_____

_____

_____

_____

_____

_____

_____

_____

Yours sincerely,

Personal Worksheet

Below is a worksheet for you to use to tell your own story of your experience with the thinking error of 'False Cause' as it happened to you.

Challenge: Why did you feel the situation was a challenge? What was so challenging about it? Why was it *your* challenge?

_____

_____

_____

_____

_____

_____

_____

_____

_____

_____

_____

Choice: Why did you make the choice you did? How did it feel?

_____

_____

_____

_____

_____

_____
_____
_____
_____
_____
_____
_____

Outcome: What was the outcome? How did it feel? What did it teach you?

_____
_____
_____
_____
_____
_____
_____
_____
_____
_____
_____

Thinking Tip:
Just because one action precedes another doesn't mean it causes the following action to happen

PERSONAL ATTACKS

A 'personal attack' can hit hard as it diverts your focus from the issue onto your ego. To successfully deal with this form of manipulation, you must use your Passion to control your emotions.

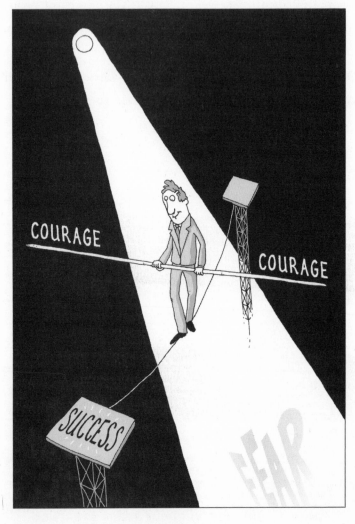

Figure 12: Courage

4) Abuse and Stereotyping – Antidote: Courage and Staying Power

As you have seen in your first steps on your 'Spiral Staircase Workout', it is most important when encountering this particular manipulation or thinking error that you use your Passion to control your emotions. This thinking error can be summed up in three words – taking things personally – and it can put you completely off track and make you lose your excellent thinking power and Passion to achieve.

When we take things personally our focus does a complete U-turn. So, instead of concentrating on our goal down the road in front of us, our focus has turned around to look at our ego pushing us on from behind. Instead of our thinking being directed ahead and focused on our goal, taking things personally makes us lose track and change focus back onto ourselves and our ability to achieve our goal. This can cause us to falter and so not achieve our aim.

Think about when you are presenting your ideas at a meeting. If you are truly focused on delivering a topic you know expertly, you believe in and are passionate enough to succeed at, then your focus will be on that issue and not on your ego. However, if you begin to think of and worry about yourself carrying out this process, or if someone asks you a question you find hard to answer or makes a personal remark about you, your focus may well change and you will begin to falter as your focus hitches itself onto your ego and away from the issue.

This is a difficult thinking error as it can happen in two ways:

- ❖ When we do it to ourselves.
- ❖ When others do it to us.

A. When we highjack our own thinking: how it occurs

It is difficult to describe when we hijack ourselves in this way, as most of the time when we take things too personally we are not aware of it and may even rationalise to ourselves that it is the right thing to do.

The best way, I have found over the years, to know when you are hijacking your own Clear-Thinking abilities is to become aware of the triggers that make you do this. This has been confirmed to me many times by course participants I have had the pleasure to work with. Most recently, one course member, Ruth, commented on how her personal trigger for taking things too personally (thereby focusing her thinking on her ego and not the issue) is when she feels excluded. So 'exclusion' or her feeling of 'being excluded' makes her defensive at meetings. A second lady in our group said that her trigger is when she makes a mistake in her presentations or group discussions. The trigger of 'being wrong' sends her into a panic and she cannot think clearly.

Being able to identify these triggers will be a great help to these two participants as their awareness gives them a nanosecond of control. They understand that it is not what is being said at a meeting that is bothering them, but their reaction to what is being said, and if they can control that reaction then they have a better chance of working successfully towards their goals. Self-awareness is a terrific thinking mechanism to give us some space to work on ourselves and so improve our own thinking when needed. For we may not have the control we would like over others, but we should always strive to have control in relation to ourselves.

It might be interesting to note here your personal triggers. What kind of perception or states of being send you into a tizzy and so take away your Clear Thinking and Focus. For example, if I were to add one of my own triggers to the list of 'exclusion' and 'being wrong', I would say an important one for me is 'lack of recognition'. If I feel I am not being recognised, or others are given recognition over and above me, that is my trigger to go into an emotional state and so have a lesser understanding of any given situation and an inability to think clearly.

What are your triggers?

_____

_____

_____

_____

_____

_____

_____

Once you have noted your triggers, I hope that even that self-awareness gives you a feeling of comfort. For if we can recognise what is bothering us, we are halfway towards finding a solution.

Guided response: to respond with confidence when you highjack your own thinking

When you are aware of what upsets you or makes you feel bad, you can go some way to acting in such a way that the situation will not arise. For example, if Ruth gets upset by 'exclusion' then she can do her utmost to be involved in what is important to her from the very start. She can express her views in a way that involves both herself and others. In my case I will demand recognition for my work by focusing on building a solid reputation with sound product knowledge and delivering a suite of products that are trademarked and patented. The situation of not being recognised then cannot arise.

So, if you find that you have a trigger that sends your thinking into a tizzy, you can choose what actions you can take to either ensure that the trigger cannot happen or that, if it happens, you have a strategy to control it _and_ your Clear Thinking.

When you read the letter below from Dawn, I would like you to consider what her thinking errors might be and how you would respond as her agony aunt. Then when you have finished writing your response, have a look at what I had to say.

Exercise

This problem situation concerns our feelings when we view the promotion of others as a slight on our own ability to succeed. This is an all-too-common problem which produces very real feelings of injustice and dissatisfaction. This is what Dawn writes:

> Dear Valerie,
>
> A colleague who was on the same level as myself recently got promoted. Without sounding like sour grapes, I don't understand why she was chosen to move up the ranks and not me. From what I can see we both do the same amount of work, generally work the same hours and get on equally well with the boss. Occasionally she works later than me (well, 'til after the boss leaves the office) but I'm a great believer in fitting in all the work you have to do within the time frame you're given. I would hate to think I've been sidelined because I use my time more efficiently!
>
> Dawn

How would you respond to Dawn?

Dear Dawn,

_____

_____

_____

_____

_____

_____

_____

_____

_____

_____

_____

_____

_____

_____

_____

_____

_____

_____

Yours sincerely,

This is my response to Dawn:

Dear Dawn,

I do sympathise with you. It is really horrible to feel that others are getting on better than we are by doing less than we do. This goes against the basic law of natural justice and indeed, against everything we are told at school and by our parents: 'If you work hard, you will get on.' So, it must be very difficult for you to be in a situation where you feel you have been sidelined like this.

But is that the case, Dawn? Do you actually know what has happened here? Do you actually know why your colleague was promoted and not you? Unfortunately, the part of your thinking that stands out most to me in this letter is your lack of understanding of the situation. You say 'I don't understand why she was chosen to move up the ranks and not me ...' you continue 'from what I can see ...' etc. It seems to me you are making judgements based only on (a) your lack of understanding and (b) your own personal, and perhaps mistaken, perception.

For example, I see only one fact in your letter, which is that both you and your colleague work at the same level. After that I am getting selective information where you are making judgements that this promotion of your colleague must be because of:

- Amount of work done
- Amount of hours worked
- Ability to get on with the boss.

Do you know if these were in fact the real criteria for her successful application?

The above criteria seem to be based on your *perception*

of what your company was looking for, but do you know if this is true? You could be making yourself unhappy because of your own lack of information and understanding.

I think to lessen your torture about this promotion, I would like you to see an HR colleague and discuss your inability to get this promotion, this time, with them. The reason I say this is that I want you to 'Ask – not Assume' in order to get to the root cause of your problem.

Dawn, I think you will feel much better if you get to the real issues behind why you did not get promoted this time (and why your colleague did). It will be good for you to know the exact competencies your company requires. There are lots more competencies besides the amount of work you have to do, how long it takes and being friendly with the boss! For example, what about:

- Clear communication
- Good influencing skills
- Time management (which you have)
- Teamwork
- Problem-solving and decision-making, and many more besides.

Sit down with this HR person and work through your career path analysis, identifying the specific competencies your company is looking for and how the work you do on a day-to-day basis can ensure that your job will match future promotion requirements. At least then you will be working from a factual basis where you will fully understand what your company is looking for and how you can give it to them.

Talking to HR is also a good idea for the reason that in case there has been an injustice in your situation, it will be instantly highlighted to HR.

I have no doubt this will make you more confident for the future and less susceptible to comparing yourself with others.

On that note, may I give you one very small last piece of advice, Dawn. For your own sense of well-being and happiness, please do not compare yourself with the best others can do. Only compare yourself with the best that you can do.

I wish you the very best,

Valerie

How did you get on? Did we differ in our responses?

You will have noticed in my response that I would like Dawn to be able to distinguish between her perception of the situation and the reality of the situation. When our own shattered ego highjacks our thoughts it may be because our perceptions – and faulty ones at that – are controlling our thinking. Our perceptions are so faulty that they can make us believe we cannot do something, or are no good at achieving what we want, when in fact we are more than capable! To have better control of the situation, our thinking needs to have a firm grasp of reality in order to focus correctly.

When you feel you are taking things too personally, ask yourself if your feelings are coming only from your perception of the situation, or if there is further evidence of real grounds for believing that you're up against an enormous challenge.

To test this, ask yourself if there are other possibilities open to you that you may have not thought about and then try to follow these leads as rationally and imaginatively as you can. It is sometimes wise to ask others around you if they see your situation in the same way that you do.

B. When others highjack your thinking: how it occurs

Have you ever noticed when you are saying something you think is quite sensible (and even inspiring) that out of nowhere another person may start attacking you, hijacking you and not the issue? They may say something like: 'What would you know about that?' Or: 'You're not long enough in this organisation to understand the real issue here.' It comes as a complete shock when this happens and often can stop your thinking in its tracks – as this form of manipulation is to make you focus on yourself, your ego and so lose focus of the issue you are discussing.

It is a good trick for someone to play if they want to stop you introducing new ideas at work or a new and difficult change strategy, and they don't have any sound argument or real evidence against you. If it works, you will begin to doubt yourself and your capabilities – which, of course, is exactly what they want.

When we don't like what someone is saying we can tend to shoot the messenger, not the message. In other words, we abuse the speaker, which is a very lazy way of winning the argument, since we don't have to bother with the content of the discussion.

The power of this trick is that, if you fall victim to it, you will get caught up in the confusion of associating your 'ego' with the 'issue'. It is very powerful and it diverts the attention of the victim. When you are on the receiving end of this, it can be totally debilitating. This type of trigger diverts your Clear Thinking away from your original goal and the logical conclusion you are trying to reach. Instead your focus becomes completely centred on your ego and its safety.

If you defend yourself against this type of attack it is doubly dangerous. I know you will say to me that it is completely human to do so, and it is. But just think for a moment – if you are now defending your ego against this type of attack, where has the issue gone? The issue has been lost in the battle. Often when people fall into this trap they feel so good at having defended themselves from attack that they fail to see they have lost the argument because they did not reach their intended goal – the new idea or the changed strategy.

Sometimes it is incredibly difficult to combat this particular trick, as its effect is almost instantaneous. And when the accuser is able to tap into a specific trait in your ego and hit it with force, then you must seriously understand what is going on to be able to think quickly on your feet and not be diverted.

Guided response – to respond with confidence when others highjack your thinking

'Always get back to the issue' is the golden mantra that you must never forget. Whenever this thinking error happens, no matter what the situation is – you must always get back to the issue. To retain your focus if you are the victim of this type of thinking error, it is good to notice that the person attacking you is in a very weak position.

What I have found most of all, while teaching this type of 'thinking on your feet' over the past twenty years, is that when I come to recognise a trick (and especially this one) I can become much more powerful in getting what I want. Instead of falling into the trap, once I recognise it for what it is, I think, 'how wonderful'. If the other party is reduced to this level of thinking, they must have absolutely no proof or evidence for what they are saying. All they are doing here is attacking my ego in an attempt to save theirs, because if they had any real evidence or argument against my ideas, they could easily say so. The fact that they are reduced to ego bashing is proof that they are without a solid foundation. So I am stronger than they are and this gives me a very powerful psychological advantage.

You can think in the same way. If your opponent had any evidence that your ideas wouldn't work or that they were flawed in some way, they could simply give you that evidence, or show you the flaw. By being reduced to ego bashing it is a clear indication that they haven't. They have no proof to argue against you, so the only thing they can do is to divert your attention instead. And I hope this knowledge makes you feel more powerful, not more confused.

If you feel yourself becoming emotional during a presentation or argument, stop, even for a split second, and you will remain calm. For this pause – no matter how small – will give you a few seconds of breathing space to gather your thoughts. However, you may say: 'I would find it so hard to stop, precisely because I am emotional', but Focus is the key here and your determination will help you.

You won't need to succeed at being unemotional about everything, but when the situation or topic is really important to you, remember the point you are trying to get across and then never forget it. Prepare well for a difficult meeting so that you will be less likely to stray off the point. Do not let others divert you. There are several ways you can do this:

- Simply ignore the abuse (remember Napoleon's famous saying: 'I never interrupt my enemy when he is making a mistake' – at least, that's how you can justify your silence to others later).

- Use humour – 'I see I'm not flavour of the month … however, the point is …'

- Defer it – 'We can discuss that matter later, the point now is …'

No matter how you deal with the situation, always get back to the issue. To reach that goal, take a deep breath, smile and carry on with clear direction towards what you want to achieve – without further diversions. Remember, you are building up your courage and staying power and they will not desert you.

Exercise

A young woman who attended a recent training course of mine told me a story that illustrates this trick superbly. Sarah believed passionately in her project and had worked very hard to create a logical defence of it. She had made an excellent PowerPoint presentation to deliver to her colleagues to persuade them to take her ideas on board. This is how she described her experience at the meeting:

> I was at the time arguing my point very clearly and with some force. I was quite happy that I knew my stuff

and I was able to put my message across like the best of them. Then, suddenly, my colleague John looked me in the eye and said, 'Sarah, you're always on the defensive.'

'No, I'm not,' I replied far too quickly, because by saying this at that moment, I became defensive – which so easily proved his point, and of course my argument was completely weakened and I found it very difficult to regain credibility within the group.

Oh dear! All of us have the same tendency as Sarah. When our ego is hit or hurt we will immediately run to its defence. Not being defensive was very important to Sarah. That was her particular button, and when pressed, she fell into the trap of saving her ego. This is what people can do to you in a discussion if they don't like what you are saying, they can very cleverly (like John) attack a certain trait in your ego that they know you will rush to defend. And if you fall for this trick, they will achieve the result they are looking for, which is to divert your attention away from the issue. In addition, by doing so, if they can unnerve you and lessen your credibility within the group, they will ensure that your goal (the one they never wanted) will not be realised.

Stop for a moment here and write down what you would say to Sarah to help her regain her focus in this situation:

_____

_____

_____

_____

_____

_____

_____

_____

_____

_____

_____

_____

How did you get on? Did you tell Sarah to ask him a question like: 'That's interesting, why do you think I'm defensive?' Or: 'That's interesting, where did you see the defensiveness in the figures we are looking at?'

It is good to ask questions. But do you notice a big difference between the two queries above?

Yes, you can see that the first question relates to Sarah's ego, while the second question is firmly focused on the issue. When we are in discussions with others in this type of meeting situation, there will be two types of conversations going on: an ego conversation and an issue conversation. It is up to you to always keep the focus on the issue conversation. If the discussion strays towards an ego conversation, you must always bring it back to the issue. That is your golden mantra for retaining Clear Focus when trying to influence others. It is not easy and that is why you will flex your muscles and build up your qualities of courage and staying power. Bringing conversations and thinking back to the issue needs an iron grip of 'staying power', with plenty of dollops of good old-fashioned determination.

Personal Worksheet

Below is a worksheet for you to use to tell your own story of your experience with the thinking errors of 'Abuse and Stereotyping' as they happened to you – either self-inflicted or inflicted by others.

Challenge: Why did you feel the situation was a challenge? What was so challenging about it? Why was it *your* challenge?

_____

_____

_____

_____

_____

_____

_____

_____

_____

Choice: Why did you make the choice you did? How did it feel?

_____

_____

_____

_____

_____

_____

_____

_____

Outcome: What was the outcome? How did it feel? What did it teach you?

_____

_____

_____

_____

_____

_____

_____

_____

_____

Thinking Tip:

Always focus on the issue – not the egos

5) FUDs (Fear, Uncertainty and Doubt) – Antidote: Courage and Staying Power

As with the personal attack of Abuse and Stereotyping, our next personal attack of FUDs can again be delivered both by ourselves and others.

A. When we frighten ourselves: how it occurs

We can instil fear, uncertainty and doubt into our own thinking, just as much as someone else can. That is to say that our own thoughts can be driven by fear, uncertainty and doubt, instead of clear and focused reasoning, and we can do ourselves harm by thinking in this way. For example, when we would like to go for a promotion, but we tell ourselves that we would be no good at the job, we are not qualified enough or we would never get the interview.

The problem with this type of thinking error is that if you are afflicted by it, your thoughts are seduced into believing your fearful emotions to be true and this happens without any real proof or evidence. If you are afraid of going for that job and you don't, therefore, pursue it, you cannot possibly know that you would be no good at it, be hopeless at the interview, etc.

The power of a FUD is not that it proves anything with real evidence you can take apart and judge to be good or bad, true or false. The power of a FUD is that you can never disprove it – as you can never prove that you would be hopeless if you do not go for it. But this thinking error takes hold of you as if it were solid reasoning describing the truth, because you will never be able to prove it wrong.

Not being able to disprove something is very influential and persuasive. Think of the Lotto slogan: 'It could be you.' This is very powerful as it does seem to be true – if you buy a ticket, you could win the Lotto. No one can disprove that and you are seduced into thinking it just might be true and therefore you end up buying many tickets. However, what is wrong with this thinking is that it does not prove that you will win the Lotto, which is what you really want to know – its power is that you cannot prove that you will not win the Lotto.

Guided response: to respond with confidence to calm your own fears

The ability to think clearly is the ability to make sense of life in such a way that we can make something of ourselves. If our thinking is more about breaking sense than making sense, we may find ourselves broken under the weight of such damaging beliefs.

For that reason I hope you will be very vigilant whenever you feel that it would be difficult for you to pursue a goal. To focus correctly, to make good sense of how you are going to achieve what you want, it is most important to be aware of what is driving your thinking. To overcome a FUD thinking error, you may have to do a reality check on your thinking. Ask yourself: 'What

Figure 13: Staying Power

is driving my belief in risk? Where is the evidence?' This knowledge will help you to develop the required qualities of courage and staying power.

Courage and staying power will give you the time to think about what you want, and most importantly, these qualities keep you focused on the end result. Their influence is to keep you in the competency thinking mode to be able to overcome any problems or issues you have to work through in order to succeed. Without them you may find yourself becoming overwhelmed by the different tasks you have to assume to reach your goal.

I remember my mother's words to me as a four-and-a-half-year-old and ask you to remember also that Focus fights your Fears.

B. When others frighten you: how it occurs

It is very important to realise that the other way that FUDs can overwhelm us is when *others* use them to frighten us away from achieving a desired outcome. This happens when a FUD is directed at you in such a way that it makes you frightened of taking the risk you need to, to achieve your goal.

For example, in the workplace this is quite a common thinking error or piece of manipulation. It occurs most often in Change Management situations, when people might be frightened to change to a new strategy or action. It takes the form of making you doubt that the action you want to take is, in fact, the correct one. For example, you may wish to implement a new idea or action plan. There is no argument against your idea as it is apparently sound. So a colleague might be reduced to saying something like: 'Okay, do go ahead with that idea, but don't come crying to me when it all goes wrong ...' or 'I will just have to say I told you so when it all goes pear-shaped ...' Notice there is not one shred of evidence in these statements that anything will go wrong or pear-shaped. So this person is not giving you any reason or evidence to believe what they are saying. However, the power of the FUD is that they don't have to – and so they can get away with very lazy thinking.

The power of the FUD is that they need only say what they have to say in such a way that *you cannot disprove* what they are saying. And because you cannot *disprove* that your idea or new plan of action might not be successful, they have planted a seed of risk in your mind that it just might not be. This can then grow and take over your thought processes. So that, instead of focusing on the goal you are trying to implement, your focus has now switched to the *risk* of taking that goal and how damaging it might be to you.

You see how it happens? It is a very insidious manipulation and can become extremely powerful. Your focus is diverted and you now use your energy focusing on possible risk rather than the potential rewards for a new idea, product or service that will succeed.

Guided response: to respond with confidence when others frighten you

This thinking error/manipulative trick can be deflated and made ineffectual very quickly. In the case of someone else doing this to you, the easiest way to stop them in their tracks is to ask them for the evidence for their great doubts or worries about risk. For example, when the person says, 'I will have to say I told you so, when this all goes wrong', you can answer, 'When *what* goes wrong? What do you think will go wrong? Can you explain to me what you think will not work here?' And then stop and wait for their response. Because if they are using a FUD they will not be able to answer you, or they will try to fudge it in some way.

To continue the conversation then and refocus on the goal, you can open a discussion with your colleague about the fears they may be *feeling* about the new implementation. Empathy is often the best way to refocus the thinking of others on achieving the goals that may frighten them.

Another way to refocus on the goal when you are the victim of a FUD is to create the worst-case scenario. This is often done in very good project management work, where, to allay fears, uncertainty and doubt on achieving the end goal, the group creates worst-case scenarios to make themselves very familiar with what may go wrong, and to create strong competencies and contingency plans to deal with these scenarios. This exercise has the added bonus of making each player in the story feel confident about achieving their aims and objectives.

A lovely example of a FUD was told to me recently by a course participant on my programme 'Critical Thinking in Action'. The story is as follows: Working for a National Banking Regulatory Authority can be quite a challenge these days, following the spectacular worldwide banking crash where regulatory authorities were severely criticised for not being quick enough to 'regulate' the bankers – which was, after all, their job. The result now is that everything the regulators do is under complete scrutiny and analysis by the national media. The Focus of the regulation employees to develop good work is now hampered by the fear that their ideas must be 'absolutely perfect' before they are made public, otherwise the media will 'crucify them'.

I have been told that currently it is very difficult to get new ideas or changes through because the normal response now is to say: 'We can't do that, what if it gets into the national papers? It would be disastrous.' This fear can never be proven to be true of course, as no employee of the authority will take the risk of trying out the new idea or plan. This kind of FUD is enough to paralyse thinking and it has to be overcome.

I asked my storyteller, 'But what do you do then? Are you not able to move forward with new ideas?'

She told me that on some occasions she finds it difficult to handle this objection. But more and more she is responding by, 'It's okay if what we are doing gets into the national newspapers. We *know* that what we are doing is correct and we have the evidence to stand by our actions and justify our arguments.'

This is indeed the best way to handle a FUD and I hope a good piece of advice for you to remember and use when needed.

As the above example is excellent in showing us how to stand up to others when they try to frighten us, the exercise below will concentrate on how to handle internal and personal fearful-thinking errors.

FUDs can harm us in our life pursuits by making us focus on our fears and allowing our thinking to be driven in a real and damaging way. Here is an example from a reader, Maeve. Read what she says and, as before, try to spot her thinking errors. Please write your own response to her, commenting on her fears and the problem she is experiencing, before you read my reply letter to her.

Exercise

Fear, uncertainty and doubt limit our options through false assumptions and preconceptions. They give us a plethora of 'negative myths' about ourselves that we can accumulate over a lifetime. For many, they result in low self-esteem, lack of confidence and a genuine belief that they cannot achieve a successful, thriving and enjoyable working life.

This is what Maeve has to say:

> Dear Valerie,
>
> I am forty-eight years old. I have been in my current job for nearly ten years but there is little chance of climbing up the ranks from where I am. My employer has been very good to me these last few years as I was faced with many health and personal problems. However, I'm curious as to what else is out there. Am I too old to be thinking about a career change?
>
> Maeve

Your response:

Dear Maeve,

_____

_____

_____

_____

_____

_____

_____

_____

_____

_____

_____

_____

_____

_____

_____

_____

_____

Yours sincerely,

This is my reply:

Dear Maeve,

Thank you for taking the time to write to me. It is very interesting to hear from an experienced, ambitious person who is so obviously interested in doing more for herself and taking more of what life has to offer her.

I say this because even though you seem to be happy in your present job, with a very kind and considerate employer, you are still itching to climb the ranks and get more out of life. You are still yearning for a career change that will fulfil your ambitions. The only thought I can see that is holding you back from this more fulfilling career is your belief that you are perhaps 'too old' – fuelling your fear, uncertainty and doubt that you can do what you want to do.

It is such a pity that you have such doubtful thoughts

about your age, Maeve. I believe it is extremely unfortunate in our 'youth culture' world that so many working women in their forties, fifties and sixties can become prone to such low self-esteem and lack of confidence, simply because of their age. You do have a problem, Maeve, but it is not your age – it is only your *negative perception* of that age – your fear, uncertainty and doubt about what your age means to you. So let's see if we can work on changing your thinking to get you to produce the positive actions you need to succeed.

First of all, let me tell you that at forty-eight years of age, you are at your peak as an experienced, competent businessperson. I know a great number of women who have left large corporations at this age to start businesses of their own. They changed career in their late forties, as they felt it was the perfect age to follow their dreams. In our forties, not only do we have the dreams of our younger years, we also have the experience to know we can fulfil these dreams in a very practical way. So, forty-eight is good, believe you me.

I thought it might be useful as well to give you the example of not only one woman or two women who have successfully developed new careers in their forties and fifties, but of three women who are thriving because they have done just that.

My first example is of a mother, Sinead, who at fifty-four years of age, when her children could fend for themselves, left her comfortable home and lifestyle to begin a hectic job working for a well-known Irish employer in the travel industry. She now travels extensively and could not be happier in her work. Speaking to me she says she is very successful in her new career, as she has brought a competence and experience to the job that younger people could not have. What her new career has given her is Confidence (with a big 'C'), freedom and the belief that she can now do *anything*. Her biggest surprise since taking up her position is the reaction of other women her age, who, she says, are just filled with such admiration for her. Unfortunately, they have not got the courage to do what she has done. They say to her, and I quote, 'I can only do this small job – not the job I really want to do.' I hope you never hear yourself saying that Maeve. And to avoid that, please take my advice and follow your instinct to better yourself now.

You have many choices. You could apply for another more satisfying job with a different employer. Yes, your present employer has been very good to you, but that should not be a reason to stay in your present job. You must not stay in your job for anyone else but yourself. If you moved to a more worthwhile position you could be enjoying the success I have outlined above.

Also, you could take this opportunity to start your own business. My second example of a successful woman who did just that is a person who moved from a large multinational organisation to set up as a sole trader in her early fifties. Yes, it is scary and very hard work, but the rewards are so good. Angela tells me her new business allows her to use the vast working experience she has built up in the way that *she* wants to use it, and for herself. She now has a very strong sense of achievement with great independence, freedom and power. Through the many business networks Angela has joined, she has met several other older women who are also doing it for themselves, and succeeding just like her.

And remember, success can carry on to well past your forties. Once your work gives you that great sense of achievement, it can stretch on to any age in your life. My third example proves that: Jane started her own business in her forties, twenty years ago, and today she continues to run a thriving business, now into her sixties. She will only retire if and when she wants to. And seeing her passion for what she does, I know that will not be any time soon.

I hope you see, Maeve, that you must follow your ambition no matter what your age, and in reading the answer to this letter, I hope that you the reader will never be frightened to do the same.

Never let the negative perceptions of fear, uncertainty and doubt cloud your judgement. Clear successful decision-making should only include the facts. Please continue to read the facts above, Maeve. Successful older women surround you. Don't put up barriers before you even try. Go for it, please.

Best wishes,

Valerie

Notice the focus of my response and how it is entirely directed at the fear, uncertainty and doubt that Maeve is feeling. My response attempts to show her all the evidence, real evidence, that exists to counter those fearful impressions.

I hope you can see that the thinking error of FUDs can really damage your ability to focus in a way that is sense-making and good for you – and not sense-breaking and bad for you.

Personal Worksheet

Below is a worksheet for you to use to tell your own story of your experience with the thinking error of 'FUDs' as it happened to you – either self-inflicted or inflicted by others.

Challenge: Why did you feel the situation was a challenge? What was so challenging about it? Why was it *your* challenge?

_____

_____

_____

_____

_____

_____

_____

_____

_____

_____

_____

_____

_____

_____

Choice: Why did you make the choice you did? How did it feel?

_____

_____

_____

_____

_____

_____

_____

_____

_____

_____

_____

Outcome: What was the outcome? How did it feel? What did it teach you?

_____

_____

_____

_____

_____

_____

_____

_____

Thinking Tip:

To get rid of the great pretenders of 'fear, uncertainty and doubt', focus on evidence, not risk

6) 'You're Wrong, so, I'm Right' – Antidote: Courage and Staying Power

How it Occurs

The third and last illustration of a form of personal attack is the syndrome 'You're wrong, so I'm right', and I believe this type of manipulation is by far the most difficult to overcome. This trick of manipulation or thinking error might not only destroy your focus 'in the moment' but it may also shatter your confidence – and completely. It is a personal attack of great intellectual savvy and can floor the victim if you are not able to spot it and regain, not only your focus, but your composure.

To remain focused when you are the victim of this trick, you will need plenty of courage and even more staying power. It might be easier to remember this trick as an 'inking error' as opposed to a '(th)inking error', as the form this manipulation takes is for someone to point out mistakes you have made in your written or presentation work and in so doing, they conclude that because you have made a mistake – because you are wrong – they must be right. It is very easy to lose focus when this happens to you as you may be drawn to the error you have made and therefore lose sight of the main body of your work, which is, most probably, excellent.

Let me explain this error to you in detail. This is how this trick might happen to you, particularly in a work context. In fact this manipulation is so serious that some people have told me they have lost contracts and important deals by losing their focus when they encountered this type of manipulation.

Imagine you are giving an important presentation to some of your colleagues or an outside agency/ client. Your audience is listening intently to you and analysing your arguments. You are going through a series of reasons why you think it is a good idea to go ahead with this new product, for example, or to introduce this new service.

There is someone in the audience who doesn't want this change, but they have no solid argument of their own to stop it being introduced. So, they listen very earnestly to you and as you give your list of reasons, they will suddenly stop you and say something like: 'Hold on a minute, those figures on page three, they're wrong. Can we go back to those, because I know for a fact they are incorrect.' (I am assuming these figures are wrong, but also that they are not the central core of your argument.)

This act alone is enough to shatter confidence. To be shown up for something, no matter how small, in front of other people is a humiliating experience and can confuse us and make us lose our focus, concentration and any ground we may have gained with the group.

What can also happen, now that everyone's attention has been drawn to the fact that there is a mistake in the figures on page three, is that an awful atmosphere may be creeping around the room and people may be thinking: 'Well, if she can't even get the figures right on page three, goodness knows how valid the rest of this is?', even though no one has yet seen the rest. This is the type of damage that can be done. Even without any further analysis of the rest of your excellent presentation of an idea or ideas, people are now having doubts and may not want to hear any more.

If your accuser sees that s/he is gaining some recognition by doing this, s/he may continue with more confidence, saying: 'Well, we can see that these figures don't add up, and really I don't think it is possible to prove that this new product will work for us; in fact this is what I thought all along. I think this is a bad idea, it is wrong.' It sounds so final and so true. But think about it for a moment. Where is the proof that this is a bad idea or that you are wrong? There is none. What has happened in this exchange of views is that your interloper has pointed out that you have a small error in your presentation, where you are trying to prove that you are right and that your idea for this new product is a good one. However, this does not prove that your idea is wrong. There is no evidence to show that your idea is wrong. There is only evidence to show that you have made a small mistake in trying to prove that it is right.

The essential point to remember is: the fact that you are not able to prove that you are right, does not mean that you are wrong. This is sometimes confusing and this is why this form of manipulation and thinking error is so powerful. In most languages, English or other, 'not right' usually means 'wrong'. But in logical thinking and analysis that is not the case. Being 'not right' can mean a simple mistake in an argument, for example a small mistake in a figure, but that mistake does not prove that your idea is wrong. You could still be right and have just made a small mistake in proving that point.

This type of attack might make you feel worthless. You may doubt yourself and other people in the room may be very concerned as well. There is a way to overcome this though, so do not fret.

Guided response: to respond with confidence

Here are some actions I have found very helpful to overcome this form of manipulation or thinking error.

Excellent preparation: to avoid this attack happening in the first place it is a good idea to be very well prepared. Whether you are showing a business plan, promoting sales products or looking for a loan from the bank, ensure no one can attack your figures or find fault with your arguments by making sure they are well thought through and well checked. It is important to do this, because there is a slight grain of truth to feeling less confident about someone who doesn't seem to be well prepared. We wonder 'if they are that sloppy about their facts and figures, maybe the rest is no good', and unfortunately that has a ring of truth about it. So, be well prepared.

Relax: even if well prepared, we are, after all, human, and we will make some mistakes. If this happens, the first thing to remember is relax, it is not the end of the world to have a small mistake in your presentation. The one positive point to never forget here is that they are listening to you. That is indeed a privilege. The number of people who go to presentations and fall asleep, talk to others, do other work and do not listen is phenomenal. So, if you have them listening to you that is a very positive acknowledgement of the importance of your work.

Acknowledge the point: you must acknowledge the

point. The worst thing that can happen when someone points out a mistake about your work is that you resort to denial. As the presenter, if you reply that those figures aren't important or argue against your attacker, you may get caught up in a very downward spiral – ego bashing ego. The easiest thing to do is to acknowledge that, yes, the figures are in fact incorrect. 'Well spotted,' you might say. 'Yes, you are absolutely correct, there does seem to be a small error [minimising the problem] in those figures. Thank you for pointing that out – I will get someone back at the office to make those corrections immediately. For the moment I would like to park them, so we can continue with the excellent analysis you are giving to my work. I would appreciate your judgement on the rest of the arguments I am putting forward. For example, you will see I have four other points here. What do you think of …?' In this way you are bringing your enemy closer, thereby making sure that they can work with you and not against you.

Take back control: now you have their attention very firmly back on developing your ideas. I am assuming that each new reason you put forward is sound and supported by good evidence so that they will agree with you. Then you can say: 'Well, now that we have agreed with all of these reasons, I think that when we reintroduce the new corrected figures to complement these reasons, we will have a stronger product than I anticipated. And that it is thanks to you [attacker] for spotting that mistake earlier on. Well done and thank you for your valuable contribution to the project.'

Won't you just feel great?

By the way, if lots of your reasons are wrong, then someone pointing this out is not using a trick. In fact, they are doing both you and your company a great service. If the information as a whole or the many reasons you are citing as evidence are incorrect, then you are very ill-prepared and, perhaps, should not be giving a presentation at all!

Here is a lovely inspirational story. It is a fable from Middle Eastern philosophy that makes us see very clearly the difference between other people telling us we are wrong, while all the time showing up their complete inability to be right.

Once upon a time a student artist, someone who thought he was very good at his profession, created a painting with which he was very happy. He put up this painting in the communal area of the Art School where many would be able to appreciate it. Beneath the painting, he wrote, 'Draw a tick where you find a mistake', and he left.

When he returned the next day, he was shocked. He could not see his painting on the canvas, all he could see were ticks everywhere. The artist was shocked and hurt. That day, when he went to his art class, he relayed the story to his teacher. His teacher listened and understood his problem. He advised his student to create the exact same painting again, but this time, instead of writing: 'Draw a tick where you find a mistake', he should write: 'If you find a mistake, please fix it', and put it back up in the same place in the same communal area of the university.

So, the artist listened to his mentor's advice and redrew the painting, writing beneath it as his teacher had said and displayed it back in the same location. He returned after a week to find that his painting was in the same place and not the slightest change had been made to it. The artist was surprised and returned to his teacher, and asked what was different this time.

His teacher replied, 'People are quick in pointing out the mistakes of others, but not many can do what you can do, therefore there were no changes to your painting.'

The moral of this story is that pointing out the mistakes of others is very easy, but to actually do the good that they do is very hard to do yourself.

Exercise
I would like you to note some of your ideas here on how you would have advised this student.

_____

_____

_____

_____

_____

_____

_____

_____

_____

_____

_____

_____

Personal Worksheet

Below is a worksheet for you to use to tell your own story of your experience with the thinking error of 'You're Wrong, so I'm Right' as it happened to you.

Challenge: Why did you feel the situation was a challenge? What was so challenging about it? Why was it *your* challenge?

_____

_____

_____

_____

_____

_____

_____

_____

_____

Choice: Why did you make the choice you did? How did it feel?

_____

_____

_____

_____

_____

_____

_____

_____

Outcome: What was the outcome? How did it feel? What did it teach you?

_____

_____

_____

_____

_____

_____

_____

_____

_____

Thinking Tip to overcome 'You're wrong, so I'm right':
Remember P.R.A.T.: Prepare, Relax, Acknowledge the point, Take back control

Tired Thinking

7) Jargon – Antidote: Big-Picture Thinking
How it Occurs

Tired thinking refers to the last grouping of three thinking errors that can distract our minds when we are trying to reach good decisions or sustainable solutions. These thinking errors are simple ones and less taxing than the previous six errors you have worked on. For this reason we can run through them quite quickly.

Tired thinking is about being lazy and not being able to see either the complexities or simplicities in any given situation. When striving for our goals, we are not able to analyse the core issue(s) we are dealing with, for example, nor are we able to produce the vital creativity and innovation that we need to create new possibilities.

Tired thinking robs us of our critical thinking faculties as we succumb to the effects of Jargon, False Comparisons and Repetition. The antidote to these three pretenders is the power of 'Big-Picture Thinking' – your ability to see past the manipulative words and images that attempt to limit your analytical and creative thinking powers. (Ironically, you may have heard the phrase 'Big-Picture Thinking' used itself as a form of jargon at many meetings when a group wishes to do anything but think. However, I am using it here

Figure 14: Concentrate on the Bigger Picture

with its legitimate meaning of the need to 'expand our thinking in order to see the greater potential in all situations'.)

Jargon can be very annoying or it can be a useful shorthand for group members who are collectively very familiar with a certain expertise, helping them to think very fast and effectively. So jargon can help you to *remain* focused or it can utterly confuse you. A rule of thumb is that you should only use jargon if everyone in the room or at the group decision-making meeting understands it, otherwise you will lose valuable time having to explain, or re-explain, your ideas to others. A more serious flaw is that the group may very well make bad decisions as some in the decision-making process do not understand the meaning of the words being used to facilitate group thinking.

Guided response: to respond with confidence

The golden rule, if you want everyone to remain focused and clearly understand what is happening, is that your words must have real meaning while you ponder actions to take – i.e. your words are clear and can be understood first time around. If there is any ambiguity about what is being said, or asked, it can cause great confusion and divert all attention away from the main issue at hand. If there is any ambiguity in a group decision-making process, the second golden rule is that it is *always* the fault of the speaker. So, if you are the speaker in a group decision-making scenario, be very careful how you use words and keep them as simple and as easy to understand as possible. If you are a listener in the group, you have the responsibility to ask questions of the speaker if you do not understand what s/he is saying.

Bad decision-making can be the result of a simple lack of understanding and is a pathetic way to fall almost at the very last hurdle of reaching your Peak Performance.

Exercise

Here is a quiz to test your powers to communicate ideas in a focused and concise way that anyone can understand.

You will be given an example using a jargon word or phrase. Your task is to rephrase the statement so that it is clear, concise and nothing more. Your challenge is to de-jargonise the statement. Answers are on page 220.

Let's see how you get on.

1. Jargon: *Think outside the box*

Example: 'In the last two fiscal years, we've used out-side-the-box thinking to facilitate best practice and maximise efficiencies.'

De-jargonise: _____

_____

2. Jargon: *End user*

Example: 'Our new website maximises interaction and efficiencies for our end users.'

De-jargonise: _____

_____

3. Jargon: *Leverage*

Example: 'We can leverage our HR staff to process these personnel files.'

De-jargonise: _____

_____

4. Jargon: *Mission-critical*

Example: 'It is absolutely mission-critical for this business that we consistently meet customer needs and expectations.'

De-jargonise: _____

_____

5. Jargon: *Siloed*

Example: 'The departments are siloed, which contributes to our chronic communication failures.'

De-jargonise: _____

_____

6. Jargon: *Push the envelope*

Example: 'Our change agents have done a great job of thinking outside the box and pushing the envelope to drive adoption of our new strategic policy.'

De-jargonise: _____

_____

So, how did you get on with this quiz?

As you can see from the above six examples and how they are when the jargon is removed, it is much easier to understand these thoughts when they are put in simple English. Communicating them through jargon gives the receivers far more work and distracts them from the goal at hand. 'Tired thinking', paradoxically, confuses us by making our thoughts and actions far too complicated. It takes a much sharper mind to keep things simple.

To finish off this section I thought you might enjoy a humorous look at an across-the-world HR policy and how jargon might work there. (I hope my HR readers will enjoy this most of all!)

You have been warned!

Human resources departments never sack or fire anyone. For example, one American company called firing staff 'a refocusing of the company's skills-set'. Here are other examples of HR-speak for firing staff:

1. Career alternative enhancement programme
2. Career-change opportunity
3. De-hiring staff

4. De-recruiting resources

5. Downsizing employment

6. Employee reduction activities

7. Implementing a skills mix adjustment

8. Negative employee retention

9. Optimising outplacement potential

10. Rectification of a workforce imbalance

11. Redundancy elimination

12. Right-sizing employment

13. Selecting out manpower

14. Strategic downsizing

15. Vocation relocation policy.

If the human resources department uses one of these phrases to fire you, take heart, you're not unemployed, you're simply 'in an orderly transition between career changes while undergoing a period of non-waged involuntary leisure during your temporary outplacement'.[8]

Personal Worksheet

Below is a worksheet for you to use to tell your own story of your experience with the thinking error of 'Jargon' as it happened to you.

---

8 Nick Wright, 'Keep it Jargon-free', www.plainlanguage.gov/howto/wordsuggestions/jargonfree.cfm

Challenge: Why did you feel the situation was a challenge? What was so challenging about it? Why was it *your* challenge?

_____

_____

_____

_____

_____

_____

_____

_____

_____

Choice: Why did you make the choice you did? How did it feel?

_____

_____

_____

_____

_____

_____

_____

_____

_____

_____

_____

Outcome: What was the outcome? How did it feel? What did it teach you?

_____

_____

_____

_____

_____

_____

_____

_____

_____

_____

_____

Thinking Tip against Jargon:
To remain focused and achieve your goals,
always keep things simple

8) False Comparisons – Antidote: Big-Picture Thinking
How it Occurs

The thinking error of False Comparisons happens when we are seduced by a brilliant example or great story to believe that something is true when it is not.

It is so easy to believe in what someone is saying because of the way they tell the story. We fall for beautiful and visual False Comparisons every time we believe in the advertisements that show us beautiful men and women and think that we can be like them if we buy the same anti-aging or beauty product they are promoting.

We fall for False Comparisons every time we cannot see the bigger picture of what is really going on – a sales and marketing story to entice us to buy a product without the value of the product being either analysed or justified. The product is sold to us by connecting us to the beautiful picture of who we would like to be/ look like.

Everyone loves these feel-good stories and it is why they are used to sell products, services and new ideas. It is easy to believe in stories that are familiar to us, with examples and comparisons we can understand and emulate. However, these stories, with their easy to understand examples, comparing what we like with the new idea that is being introduced or sold to us, are a manipulation of our thinking and can lead us to false conclusions.

For example, again in advertising, you will often notice the use of infants or baby animals in the sales pitch. This connection invariably causes consumers to rank the potential purchases higher in sincerity, because they associate infancy with innocence and honesty, and so believe the product being sold has those same qualities as well. However, *comparing* or connecting oneself with honesty or innocence, does not make one either innocent or honest.

This kind of manipulation is so attractive that we can easily miss it. We like it as it makes it easier to think through the best options available to us when we are searching for answers. It also helps to communicate things easily and effectively. And it has done substantial damage in business organisations down through the ages.

Historically, many people have focused utterly on bad ideas because of good stories through power and media manipulation. Conversely, many good ideas have not even seen the light of day because of the dull way in which they have been introduced. It is not uncommon for many very worthwhile recommendations to be lost because of the dullness of the reports in which they are written. The ideas are not championed, they are not brought alive in order to allow others to grasp them and to focus on them long enough for them to become meaningful. So the fault can lie with the story being too seductive or not seductive enough. The comparisons, examples and analogies (or lack thereof) distort the true meaning and value of what is being communicated.

And of course this is very important for all of us in today's very competitive business environment. We are in the workplace generating new ideas, introducing changes, sometimes on a daily basis, and trying our best to retain peak performance in all we do. At meetings we are constantly jostling with each other to gain acceptance for new ways.

For example, imagine in your workplace you are trying to introduce a new idea and there is someone in the room who doesn't want this to happen. They can easily turn to you, especially if you are new, and say something like, 'There is no use introducing this new idea. We tried a similar function a few years ago and it failed miserably.' This can sound very plausible and quite logical and you could well be taken in by the pseudo-logic of this statement. However, it is an example of a False Comparison as, unless this person can show the evidence, there is as yet no connection between your idea and the one that failed a few years ago. Simply *saying* they are both similar does not *prove* that they are. For this comparison to be true there must be hard evidence put on the table.

If you are ever in a position where you are comparing your ideas with someone else's, or with previous ones, it is imperative that you do not fall for False Comparisons. They are very seductive and because they come in the form of a story, they are often very believable and, like jargon, can make us completely bypass our critical thinking faculties. That is, we are unable to judge the real value of a new idea or product, based on strong evidence and valid reasoning, because we are so taken in by the dazzling comparisons and examples in which it is wrapped.

Guided response: to respond with confidence

The way to overcome False Comparisons or analogies is quite easy:

1. Analyse the comparison to spot similarities and differences. If you are not aware of them, seek or ask for such evidence. In this way you can show up the False Comparison by pointing out there are in fact more differences than similarities.

   For example, in the workplace scenario above, where you were told that you could not introduce a new practice or idea because they did it a few years ago and it failed miserably, you can point out that today's situation is *completely different* from that of a few years ago. In showing the very great differences you will also be building up a good argument to show why it *will* work today, because there is no comparison between the present economic environment and that of a previous time.

2. A second method of overcoming a False Comparison is to ask for valid evidence. If someone is pressing you to make a decision by comparing their new idea in a favourable way with its successful implementation in another company, for example, ask the person to give you solid evidence for their beliefs, with facts and figures to back up their proposition. Make it clear to them that you cannot make a decision simply by hearing favour-

able comparisons between the new idea and the success of others.

This allows you to show the speaker that you appreciate their efforts and you would simply like to have more knowledge and evidence to believe in their ideas. It will make them think at a deeper level and perhaps this action alone will help them to find further and more substantial evidence for their new idea or project.

Exercise

Here are five simple examples of False Comparisons and analogies. Can you explain why they are wrong? The answers are on pages 220–1.

1. Medical Student: 'No one objects to a physician looking up a difficult case in medical books. Why, then, shouldn't students taking a difficult examination be permitted to use their textbooks?'

2. People who have to have a cup of coffee every morning before they can function have no less a problem than alcoholics who have to have their alcohol each day to sustain them.

3. To say humans are immortal is like saying a car can run forever.

4. Because human bodies become less active as they grow older and eventually die, it is reasonable to expect that political bodies will become less and less

active the longer they are in existence, and that they, too, will eventually die.

5. Mind and rivers can both be broad. It is a known fact that the broader the river, the shallower it is. Therefore it must be true that the broader the mind is, the shallower it is.

Personal Worksheet

Below is a worksheet for you to use to tell your own story of your experience with the thinking error of 'False Comparisons' as it happened to you.

Challenge: Why did you feel the situation was a challenge? What was so challenging about it? Why was it *your* challenge?

_____

_____

_____

_____

_____

_____

_____

_____

_____

_____

_____

Choice: Why did you make the choice you did? How did it feel?

_____

_____

_____

_____

_____

_____

_____

_____

Outcome: What was the outcome? How did it feel? What did it teach you?

_____

_____

_____

_____

_____

_____

_____

_____

_____

Thinking Tip to combat False Comparisons:
Don't be seduced by a good story – always ask for proof or evidence

9) Repetition – Antidote: Big-Picture Thinking

How it Occurs

Repetition is our last thinking error and it is probably the most infuriating. Someone constantly repeating themselves or their ideas, without any justification, manipulates us.

To remain focused to achieve your goals you need to be able to justify what you are thinking, the choices you want to make and the decisions you will act upon. If you keep repeating only what you want, without justification, and if others keep repeating what they want, without justification, then there is every possibility that you will all come to incomplete or erroneous conclusions or actions.

This is what propaganda is about for example – the endless repetition of one side or view of the world. Propaganda is usually repeated and dispersed over a wide variety of media to create a persuasive result of belief in the attitude of an audience.

People will endlessly repeat themselves in an attempt to persuade you that they are the good guys or that they know what they are talking about. This can happen in all organisations for which we work. Internal propaganda is often the life force of many meetings!

However, all we do when we repeat ourselves is to reinforce what we are saying. We do not justify it in any way or give any evidence to prove our point. This is frustrating, as often when statements are made again and again in a confident manner without argument or proof, we tend to believe them quite independently of the presence or absence of evidence for their truth. Again, we tend to accept these statements more readily if someone famous or of great celebrity utters them. And the more familiar a statement is to us, the more likely we are going to believe it – without proof.

You will notice that advertising is all about repetition. The more you see a product, the more likely you are going to buy it (they call it 'brand awareness'). However, simple repetition does not give you any evidence to believe in the product. The power of suggestion is in the repetition.

Repetition is a dangerous thinking error and one that we need to be careful of so as not to lose Focus as we reach our Peak Performance. This is why I despair a little when I hear of people being motivated by 'positive thinking' because of its endless repetition. We are told to believe in the viability of these positive thoughts to achieve the results we want by focusing on their endless repetition. Simply repeating a wish over and over again may indeed focus you on the 'ideal' you want to reach, but it doesn't allow your critical thinking faculty to focus on the good ideas you will need to produce to bring about the reality you so desire.

In fact the thinking error of believing that repetition alone can achieve our goals is, I would argue, a form of lazy thinking, or just being lazy, full stop. In terms of Clear Thinking and Focus, it is confusing the two concepts of 'ideal' and 'idea'. When we think that all we have to do to achieve what we want is to really believe in it and it will appear to us, we are confusing an 'ideal' with the hard work involved in attaining an 'idea' to make it happen.

Let me explain what I mean. An 'ideal' is an aspiration, it is something we wish for as human beings. Everyone wants to have the ideal life – the ideal marriage, the ideal career, the ideal family, etc. Many of our moral beliefs and practical ambitions, such as goodness and truth as well as beauty and good fortune, are ideals. However, we cannot achieve these simply by envisioning them, repeating that we want them or praying for them, without adding in just a little bit of hard work. In order to avoid the repetitive standstill of wishful thinking and so progress to achieving our ideals, we need to use our critical and creative thinking faculties to come up with good 'ideas' to make the 'ideals' happen.

Ideas are actions, the know-how to make our ideals become reality. If ever you think you have a good idea, always check if you know how to make it happen. If you don't know what action to take to make your idea happen, then it is not an 'idea', it is only an 'ideal'. We cannot bring an ideal into reality. An ideal is a concept. The only way you can bring the aspiration of 'goodness' into the world is if you know how to be good – if you can carry out good acts. The magic word that transforms an 'ideal' into an 'idea' is the word *how*.

I always say to course participants in the workshops we run: 'If you are at a meeting and you believe you are hearing good ideas, never let anyone out of the room unless they know *how* they are going to produce those ideas in action.' For if we don't know what actions we are going to take, or need to take, to bring an idea into reality, then it is not an idea, but only an ideal – an aspiration. And no matter how many times we repeat the greatness of this 'idea' it will never happen as it is not fully thought through. There is only endless repetition of the ideal, without any justification or reality check on how it can be achieved.

Guided response: to respond with confidence

The easy thing to remember with repetition is not to believe in it. Ask for evidence and proof. If a group or organisation claims to be the best, make them prove it, don't let them just repeat it. Don't be taken in by how many times you see their name, or how many famous people buy their product. If they want to sell to you, make sure the product will be effective in satisfying *your* needs.

If you find you are the victim of repetition – or tired thinking – ask the person or group two simple questions:

- Why? – for justification.
- How? – for action.

And then sit back and listen ...

If you are in a discussion with someone and they keep repeating how wonderful they are in so many different ways, ask them to prove it by doing something. Actions speak far louder than words.

If you find you are using this thinking error yourself, acknowledge that what you desire is an aspiration and then go out and do something about getting it. Perform real actions that require real, gutsy thinking. Leave the wishful thinking for Cinderella and enjoy focusing on your much bigger picture. Concentrate on the illustration opposite to remind you of your ability to achieve your own wisdom.

Exercise

Think of a goal you dearly wished for and have achieved. Write down your ideal – your aspiration – and then list the number of ideas you came up with to make that goal a reality.

IDEAL: _____

IDEAS I produced – actions I successfully pursued to achieve my ideal:

_____

_____

Figure 15: A Recipe for Wisdom

_____

_____

_____

_____

_____

Now write down a goal you dearly wish to achieve but have not been able to do so.

IDEAL: _____

Take a moment to relax and brainstorm as many ideas as you can come up with to make your ideal a reality.

IDEAS I can action to achieve my goal:

_____

_____

_____

_____

_____

_____

_____

Your task is to check how 'doable' these ideas are. If they are not real actions you can achieve, then you are only telling yourself what you think you should do and not necessarily what you can or even want to do. To stop this 'thinking repetition' or 'wishful thinking' try to work on how you can change your ideas into real actions to get what you want. You know you can do it as you have the proof of your success in the first part of this exercise.

Personal Worksheet

Below is a worksheet for you to use to tell your own story of your experience with the thinking error of 'Repetition' as it happened to you.

Challenge: Why did you feel the situation was a challenge? What was so challenging about it? Why was it *your* challenge?

_____

_____

_____

_____

_____

_____

_____

_____

_____

_____

Choice: Why did you make the choice you did? How did it feel?

_____

_____

_____

_____

_____

_____

_____

_____

_____

_____

Outcome: What was the outcome? How did it feel? What did it teach you?

_____

_____

_____

_____

_____

_____

_____

_____

_____

_____

Thinking Tip to Fight Repetition:
Always ask for justification of an idea – don't allow endless repetition

YOUR THIRD AND FINAL STOP: THE 'PERSEVERANCE' PLATFORM

It is now time to rest on your last and third platform of the spiral staircase. This is again a place where you can relax, put down your reading and reflect on how you can implement the ideas you have just digested as you have worked your way from Focus, through Clear Thinking to successful Influence.

As you take your rest, you can reward yourself for all you have done so far in reading this book. You have committed to understanding not only the first skill of using your Passions to control your emotions, but you have also added the second and more difficult skill of turning negative thinking into positive action, and in these last steps you have 'run the marathon' with regard to Clear Thinking and Focus. You have digested the nine most common thinking errors and forms of manipulation, and worked through the exercises and engagements of how they can occur. With this added knowledge you now have the ability not only to think clearly, but also to influence others around you – because you have the ability to keep your head while all around are losing theirs!

It is time to reflect on what you have read and how it can help you in your life. You now have the power to remain focused and to achieve what you want. You are aware of what helps and hinders Focus and so you can call on those skills and avoid what may make you fail.

It is now all about your determination and how much you want to succeed.

PEAK PERFORMANCE: USING YOUR POWER

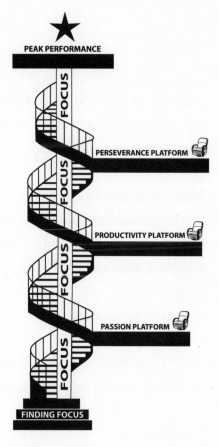

Taking the last few steps to your Peak Performance is no longer a learning curve. You can walk very easily and proudly up these last steps as they give you the space to affirm what you already know and have learned. Each last step is the way to your full potential.

These last steps are pointers for you to remember the three most important strengths of Focus that I wrote about at the very beginning of this book:

- Focus fights your Fears
- Focus is Fun
- Focus is Forever

The four-and-a-half-, six- and eight-year-old child that I was then, and the adult I am today, want you to remember how important Focus is to you reaching your highest potential.

You have the power to focus on what you want, and to achieve it guided by the skills found in this book. You have the power to be at your best 'in the moment' when you most need to be. You have the power to be who you want to be.

Here are your reminders on how to reach your Peak Performance.

By using your POWER in the following way you will have Clear Focus to Influence and Succeed:

P: *Passion*

You will be passionate, never emotional.

O: *Ownership*

You will own your idea(s) at all times no matter how many obstacles you may meet. You know you have the power to overcome them.

W: Willpower

Your willpower is a muscle and you know how to flex it when you need to.

E: Empowerment

With your three powers above, you feel empowered to achieve what you want.

R: Resilience

Finally, you have the resilience to achieve your goal. You understand manipulation and you have the resilience to overcome it to reach the results you require.

Clear Thinking is essential to you achieving and sustaining your POWER and it is perhaps fitting to remind ourselves of its great importance with the following quote from Professor William Lyons:

The frightening thing is not the thought of death, but the death of thought.

(from his play Wittgenstein (The Crooked Roads), 2010)

I hope you enjoyed reading this book, working with me through the exercises and flexing your thinking and willpower muscles. My dearest wish is that they will allow you to achieve your most cherished dreams.

To end, I offer you this reflection. It is a poem by the talented artist and writer Deborah Chock (she has a great gallery on Place des Vosges, Paris, if you can visit), which allows you to question where your real power is coming from.

Par Foi,

les fées

nous aiment

D'Autres fois

La Magie Sienne est lá

L'Âme agit

Encore

Et en corps

(Deborah Chock, 2007)

This is a play on words for all of you who want to do it 'your way'.

If we believe in them (*Par foi*)	Sometimes (*Parfois*)
The fairies (*les fées*)	The fairies (*les fées*)
Love us (*nous aiment*)	Love us (*nous aiment*)
Other times (*D'Autres fois*)	Other times (*D'Autres fois*)
The magician is there (*le Magicien est lá*)	It is our own personal magic (*la Magie Sienne est lá*)
The Soul reacts (*L'Âme agit*)	That makes our Soul react (*L'Âme agit*)
Again (*Encore*)	Again (*Encore*)
and in our body (*et en corps*)	and in our body (*et en corps*)

(Translation by Valerie Pierce, 2013)

May I wish you the very best of good luck with your most essential thoughts. I hope they allow you to sustain a focused, happy and influential life with others.

Answers to Quizzes

Jargon quiz

1. *Think outside the box* – De-jargoned: 'We have become better at working more efficiently.'
2. *End user* – De-jargoned: 'Our new website is easier for customers to use.'
3. *Leverage* – De-jargoned: 'We can use our HR staff to process these personnel files.'
4. *Mission-critical* – De-jargoned: 'This business has to satisfy its customers or it will go under.'
5. *Siloed* – De-jargoned: 'Our departments are isolated and don't share information, which damages the company.'
6. *Push the envelope* – De-jargoned: 'We went further than anyone ever has in testing how much work our team could do.'

False Analogies quiz

1. Medical Student: 'No one objects to a physician looking up a difficult case in medical books. Why, then, shouldn't students taking a difficult examination be permitted to use their textbooks?'

   Explanation: The two situations are completely different. One is to aid in patient diagnosis: the other is meant to test the analytical and memory skills of the student in examination.

2. People who have to have a cup of coffee every morning before they can function have no less a problem than

alcoholics who have to have their alcohol each day to sustain them.

Explanation: Coffee and alcohol are not comparable as two types of drinks in their effects on the person.

3. To say humans are immortal is like saying a car can run forever.

Explanation: There is no similarity between a human and a car.

4. Because human bodies become less active as they grow older and eventually die, it is reasonable to expect that political bodies will become less and less active the longer they are in existence and that they, too, will eventually die.

Explanation: The word 'body' may be the same, but it has two entirely different meanings in 'human body' and 'political body' which are not comparable.

5. Mind and rivers can both be broad. It is a known fact that the broader the river, the shallower it is. Therefore it must be true that the broader the mind is, the shallower it is.

Explanation: Mind and rivers are totally different from each other. Comparing them doesn't make any sense.

ACKNOWLEDGEMENTS

I would like to acknowledge the assistance of some great people who helped me in so many different ways when writing this book.

FOR THE SUPPORT
I would like to acknowledge the support of my family and friends who were a sounding board for the ideas in this book. I thank them for their sound judgement, support and confidence in my ability to be meaningful. Special recognition must go to Cousin Anne, who produced wonderful dinners on many difficult summer evenings when I struggled to complete this writing.

FOR THE INSPIRATION
I would like to thank my cherished clients who have given me so many invaluable examples of their strong ability to focus and to achieve their goals. I particularly thank my very helpful focus group for giving me great insights into how best to direct this book to the needs of you, the reader.

FOR THE CREATION
I cannot forget to thank my team of publishers at Mercier Press. To Dominic who was the inspiration for the Spiral Staircase metaphor that runs through

this book and to the many tireless editors on the team who directed my writing to the standard of success it is today.

PRACTICAL ASSISTANCE AND FOLLOW-UP

Valerie Pierce is an international training consultant & coach who delivers programmes on the topic of 'Clear & Critical Thinking'. Her courses run throughout Ireland, the UK, Europe and the USA.

For further information, see her website:
www.clearthinkinginaction.com

QUICK THINKING ON YOUR FEET
VALERIE PIERCE

978 1 85635 409 7

Success, both in business and in everyday life, depends on clear and effective thinking – especially under pressure. Whatever your purpose, how you think about it will determine your success. *Quick Thinking On Your Feet* will show you how to strengthen your thinking techniques and so improve the quality and productivity of your work – you will be able to work smarter rather than harder.

www.mercierpress.ie